SAVING MY FIRST KISS

SAVING MY
first kiss

why i'm keeping
confetti in my closet

LISA VELTHOUSE

Regal

From Gospel Light
Ventura, California, U.S.A.

PUBLISHED BY REGAL BOOKS
FROM GOSPEL LIGHT
VENTURA, CALIFORNIA, U.S.A.
PRINTED IN THE U.S.A.

Regal Books is a ministry of Gospel Light, a Christian publisher dedicated to serving the local church. We believe God's vision for Gospel Light is to provide church leaders with biblical, user-friendly materials that will help them evangelize, disciple and minister to children, youth and families.

It is our prayer that this Regal book will help you discover biblical truth for your own life and help you meet the needs of others. May God richly bless you.

For a free catalog of resources from Regal Books/Gospel Light, please call your Christian supplier or contact us at 1-800-4-GOSPEL *or* www.regalbooks.com.

Originally published by Servant Publications in 2003.

All Scripture quotations, unless otherwise indicated, are taken from *Holy Bible, New International Version®*. Copyright © 1973, 1978, 1984 by International Bible Society. Used by permission of Zondervan Publishing House. All rights reserved.

Other versions used are
NLT—Scripture quotations marked (NLT) are taken from the *Holy Bible*, New Living Translation, copyright © 1996. Used by permission of Tyndale House Publishers, Inc., Wheaton, Illinois 60189. All rights reserved.

Although the men and women whose stories are told in this book are real, all names (except my family's names) have been changed to protect privacy.

Cover design by PAZ Design Group, Salem, Oreg.

Library of Congress Cataloging-in-Publication Data

Velthouse, Lisa, 1981–
  Saving my first kiss : why I'm keeping confetti in my closet / Lisa Velthouse.
    p. cm.
  Originally published: Ann Arbor, Mich. : Servant Publications, 2003.
  ISBN 0-8307-3487-2
  1. Young women—Religious life. 2. Young women—Conduct of life. 3. Dating (Social customs)—Religious aspects—Christianity. I. Title.

BV4551.3.V45 2004
248.8'33—dc21   2004000113

1 2 3 4 5 6 7 8 9 10 11 12 13 14 15 / 09 08 07 06 05 04

Rights for publishing this book in other languages are contracted by Gospel Light Worldwide, the international nonprofit ministry of Gospel Light. Gospel Light Worldwide also provides publishing and technical assistance to international publishers dedicated to producing Sunday School and Vacation Bible School curricula and books in the languages of the world. For additional information, visit www.gospellightworldwide.org; write to Gospel Light Worldwide, P.O. Box 3875, Ventura, CA 93006; or send an e-mail to info@gospellightworldwide.org.

DEDICATION

To my parents, **Ben and Faye Velthouse,**
for sending flowers on Valentine's Day.

CONTENTS

THANKS TO:

Whoever invented the Track Changes on my computer. I am eternally grateful.

Crystal Rounce and Craig Coe for letting me miss work. (I owe you big.)

The staff at *Brio* magazine for having a vision and for giving me a place to jump from.

My professors for letting me work on my book and turn in assignments late.

Brad Lampe of Synergy Photography for your support and your fatherly encouragement. (I promise I'll come back!)

All those who graciously lent me their stories.

The women who keep me sane and tell me which paragraphs to cut out: Alyssa, Becky, Doni, Heather, Katie, Kim, Kristy, Linda, Mandy, Mandy, Nicole, Pam, Sara, Sarah, Shannon, and Terry.

Christina Freed for making me laugh, for putting up with my "hermitage," and for being my sounding board.

Dr. Mary Brown for helping me get started, for helping me to keep going, for understanding everything, and for letting me cry in your office.

The staff at Servant Publications for answering all of my ignorant e-mails, for tolerating my naiveté, and for believing in this project from the start.

My family at Central Wesleyan Church for your prayers and for asking how things were going. Special thanks to the following "core": the Davises, the Ertmans, the Facklers, the Hontzes, the Kruithoffs, the Lubbens, the Nienhuises, the Overbeeks, the Sprows, the VanDykes, the VanNoords, and the VerWyses.

The Seaborns and the Topps for being second families to me and for modeling Christ in your relationships.

My family—both extended and immediate—for your encouragement, consistency, and honesty. Special thanks to my parents and siblings, Ben and Faye, Noah, Sarah, and David Velthouse, for enduring the (very) rough drafts and a writer who is just as rough at times.

The man of my dreams—even if you're just a figment of my imagination. Waiting for you keeps me going.

My Lord and Savior. Thank You for creating love and language. Remind me that I do not deserve Your grace. Remind me how to live in the dust of Your sandals. Remind me that I am, first and foremost, *Yours*.

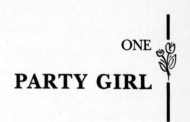

ONE

PARTY GIRL

Be joyful always.... Give thanks in all circumstances, for this is God's will for you in Christ Jesus.

1 THESSALONIANS 5:16, 18

This is exactly why shopping carts were invented, I thought, glancing down at the load between my arms. A heap of noisemakers had built up at the crook of my elbow, and my left pinkie alone held three packages of balloons. Two other fingers on that hand balanced four rolls of streamers, stacked up like the Leaning Tower of Pisa.

Peeking at the people around me, I couldn't stop the mischievous grin that was spreading across my face.

Honestly, Lisa, I thought, suddenly feeling a little unsure of myself, *this is ridiculous.* I looked like a one-woman circus sideshow.

In an attempt to regain some of my dignity, I reached for my final purchase of the day: a bag of paper hats with smiley faces all over them. Very dignified, indeed.

I was determined to appear at least somewhat balanced while leaving the decorations aisle, so I moved to transfer a few of the items from my left side to my right. With that, one package of streamers fell off its steady little stack and rolled down the aisle. By crunching the rest of my items against me and walking slightly pigeon-toed, I was able to catch up with it. So much for poise and stability.

Stooping to retrieve the little runaway, I couldn't help but let out a private laugh. *Seriously, this is so pitiful,* I thought.

More carefully then, and somewhat less pigeon-toed, I maneuvered myself toward the front of the store. Upon reaching an empty checkout lane, I plopped my load of goods down in front of the cashier and smiled pathetically. Then, just as I thought things couldn't get much worse, they did.

With a slight glance at the pile on the conveyor belt in front of her, the young woman asked, "Birthday party?"

Well, to be honest, I hadn't expected anyone to ask me *that* question. I shook my head like a total idiot and then tried to justify the mound of decorations between us.

"No, it's not ...," I said. Not knowing what else to say, I let my voice trail off.

If there was ever a time in my life when I felt more brainless than I did at that moment, I certainly cannot think of it. The cashier was looking at me with question marks in her eyes, trying to sort through my meaningless words. I remained voiceless and motionless, avoiding eye contact at all costs. Then, after a large amount of stammering, I went on.

"Um ... we're having a big party at my house, but we're not really sure when it will be." I offered a smile that was just as weak as my explanation had been.

The young woman's puzzled expression didn't go away—but I was not about to tell her anything more. Instead I pretended to be very interested in watching her scan purchases into the computer. She finished totaling my items and put them all in a white plastic shopping bag, while I endured a few more seconds of humiliation. I then handed over $10.63, grabbed my receipt and the bulging sack, and left the store.

I rolled my eyes sheepishly, wondering what the cashier thought about me and my armload of party supplies. To this day I laugh when I imagine what the young woman would have said if she had known that I was planning a First Kiss Party.

The Birth of My Insanity

Yeah, yeah, I know, this is not normal. I fully understand that it is bizarre, peculiar, and even a bit creepy. But what else is a girl supposed to do?

For as long as I can remember, you see, I have been a hopeless romantic—a starry-eyed, mushy, blubbering, wistful, head-in-the-clouds romantic. I'm a huge fan of love notes, poems, and serenades. The sight of a dozen red roses makes me grin, even if the flowers are for someone else.

I read bridal magazines for the sole reason that they bring me joy, and I am convinced that nothing is more fun than thinking about the man of my dreams. In my lifetime I've witnessed three proposals, and I have sighed with joy each time the lucky girl said "yes." (In one instance I even jumped up and down.)

Up until the time I went shopping for my party supplies, I had always considered romance to be an indispensable part of living. Despite that fact, romance had, for the most part, eluded my personal life up to that point. Since my whirlwind relationship with Ross Bradley in the fourth grade, I had not had a boyfriend. Despite all my eyelash-batting, I graduated from high school wondering if I would ever get the chance to go out with a guy.

As a romantic to the core, the fact that love hadn't come my way was not easy for me to deal with. The reality that I hadn't dated was completely mortifying to me—so embarrassing that I would hardly speak about the subject. Often I avoided even thinking about it because it could make me sick to my stomach.

From my perspective, an existence without dating was almost the worst thing that could have happened to me. Almost.

You see, as bad as it was that I hadn't dated, there was one thing that made my life even worse: I had never been kissed. Not once, not even with a stolen smooch on the playground.

Something to Cheer About

The great poet Lord Byron once said, "Man's love is of man's life a thing apart," but "'tis woman's whole existence."

I couldn't agree more. Sometimes it feels as if I *live* to experience romance. Things like dates and hugs and holding hands carry a special significance for me. Even Valentine's Day gets a particular piece of my heart. Still, as significant as those things are, none of them can compare to a single smooch.

Even *I* know that a girl's first kiss is monumental. When Sally got smooched behind our garage in first grade, it was a *huge* deal. Each time one of my girlfriends got her first kiss, I heard about it within hours (thanks to those middle school and high school gossip chains). And some of the best-ever movie scenes revolve around a first kiss or almost-kiss.

If nothing else, your first kiss entitles you to a week's worth of bragging rights among all of your friends. My senior year of high school, smack in the middle of cheerleading season, one of the girls on my squad was dating a star basketball player. The two of them were *the* couple in my school at the time, and we cheerleaders would ask our teammate about her budding relationship at almost every practice and game. Whether we were sitting on bleachers during a break or stretching out on a gym floor, one of us would bring the subject up.

"Has he kissed you yet?" we'd ask, and our snooping ears would wait in expectation to see if the two had made it "official." After a few weeks of waiting and wondering, it happened. He kissed her, she told us, and we looked at their relationship in a whole new light: They were headed in the same direction—together.

So in my own life, more than just the fact that I had never been kissed, my maiden mouth let me know that I had never been part of a *real* romantic couple. I had never felt accepted, honored, or chosen by a guy, and that made me feel as if I was traveling in the slow lane all by myself. I longed to go out on dates, to be kissed, and to feel loved by someone of the opposite sex, but none of those things were happening in my life.

Why weren't they?

Excuses, Excuses

My first try at a response to that question was that there was something dreadfully wrong with me. Did I smell funny? Did people think I had an incurable disease? Was there something in my teeth?

In attempts to persuade myself otherwise, I came up with ingenious excuses as to why I had not dated, why I had not been asked out, and why I had not been kissed. From September to late March of every year, I claimed that I was just too busy with cheerleading to be dating. For those months, of course, the hundreds of guys who must have *wanted* to ask me out knew me well enough to understand that I just couldn't fit them into my schedule.

When the month of April came around and cheerleading was over, I was forced to get a little more creative with my excuses—and believe me, I came up with some great ones. For example, I assured myself that guys my age were simply not mature enough for a girl like me. What's more, the guys who were a few years older than I were my brother's friends, and *everybody* knows that you can't date any of your brother's friends.

Or your brother's friend's friends.

Or the friend of your brother's friend's friend.

Ah, I was the queen of excuses to make myself feel better about my dating status. Occasionally someone would even help me out by saying something like, "Lisa, your high standards probably intimidate guys." I could milk a statement like that for weeks!

When one excuse no longer worked for me, I simply came up with another reason to account for my singleness. Each one worked for a little while, but none of them could keep my doubts away forever. The same gnawing questions were always inside me: *Is there anyone in the world who could ever love me? Will this pounding in my chest ever find another heart to beat alongside?*

Other questions were equally haunting: *Will my lips remain as they are—untouched—forever? IS there something wrong with me? If so, can it be fixed? Or am I simply unkissable, undesirable, and unlovable?*

A thousand fears and raw emotions flooded my head right along with these questions. I felt lonely. I felt unsatisfied. I felt ugly. I felt unwanted.

At nineteen years old, I had received almost no validation from the opposite sex, and I craved it more than words can express. I longed for a guy to recognize some worth in me, to make me feel I was a desirable young woman.

But not one guy had, and I often wondered if anyone ever would. I wanted to believe that acknowledgment and love existed somewhere in my future, but nothing in my present life would allow me to even imagine such a scenario.

My Big Secret

At that point I had already memorized endless Bible verses and heard hundreds of sermons about how God cared for me as no one else could. And although I believed that God loved me, I didn't really feel that was adequate. After all, God loves *everybody*— no matter how tall, short, plump, thin, nice, mean, whatever.

I wanted to know that I was good enough for a *guy*, a *human*. I wanted a great guy to choose me out of all the other young women on the planet and fall in love with me. I wanted to know that I was pretty enough, smart enough, fun enough— *enough* to be picked out of the masses. And even though the Bible told me that I was created in God's image and that I was fearfully and wonderfully made, I still was very aware that I wasn't getting picked.

As I felt my relationship status with the opposite sex dwindling, my self-esteem dwindled as well. Eventually my sense of worth got to the point where only one thing could have made me feel worse: if anyone else had known the truth.

If *anyone* had found out that I hadn't dated or hadn't been kissed, I would have been completely shattered. Somehow, keeping that history to myself made it easier to bear. If nobody else knew my story, then I wouldn't have to worry that people would bring the subject up and force my hurts to conversation's surface.

And so the secret sat within me. I told no one about my unkissed lips or my dating inexperience. Not even my closest friends were aware of the huge skeleton that was in my closet. I hadn't divulged any real details to my family either.

I knew the facts, though, and that was enough to drive me crazy.

Because I hadn't told anyone my secret, all of my embarrassment began to pile up. Day after day and week after week, my mass of emotional junk grew until there was an enormous heap of unspoken shame inside me. Like layers of garbage in a landfill, my years of bottled-up pain and hidden grief were rotting away, decomposing my self-esteem and spoiling my confidence.

Then everything changed.

The Time to Tell

It was early winter of my first year at college when I finally dared to reveal the secret that I had kept for so long. Even then I was petrified about what people might say or think in response to my news, but it was time.

I decided that Kayla, Carmen, Laura, and Julia would be the first people I told. They were my closest friends at the time, and I reasoned that I could trust them with my deepest, darkest secret.

Carefully searching for the appropriate moment to share the oh-so-intimate information, I waited. Then one day, as the five of us were sprawled around Kayla and Carmen's dorm room, our chatter conveniently led into my earth-shattering announcement.

One of the girls began talking about her first kiss, which unleashed a chain reaction of stories and memories from the others. Julia's big moment had occurred a few years before, she told us, in what I considered to be the most perfect atmosphere that was humanly possible.

Carmen's story was not nearly as romantic in my opinion, but it was good enough: in a parking lot after a date. But *hers* had happened when she was a freshman in *high school.* Here I was a freshman in college, and I had less to talk about than she could have shared four years earlier!

Continuing around our circle, Laura gave the account of *her* first kiss. "Believe it or not," she said, "mine was after a huge fireworks show. I didn't really expect it then, but it just happened, you know."

Actually, I had no clue, and I'm sure that my face fell with the very thought. Were they *trying* to make this as horrible as possible for me?

I didn't have time to revel in my misery, because The Dreaded Thing happened next: My four wonderful friends turned to hear the detailed events of *my* story. It was my moment, and I was terrified.

The Confession

For one hesitant second I doubted if I should share the secret that I was so desperately clinging to. It was just too personal, I thought, and they obviously wouldn't understand how much it hurt me. Besides, why would I want to open myself up for more pain and humiliation?

What a frenzied mess I had become!

One side of my conscience was advising me to just share with a few friends and finally get past the whole situation: *Why don't you dare to tell anyone?* it said. *You know you need to get over this! Look at yourself. You're ashamed to the point that you don't even dare to tell those who are closest to you. Honestly, do you really want this to keep eating away at you inside?*

The other side of my conscience was less composed as it frantically argued reasons why I should *not* tell anyone: *It's not that big of a deal. You can work this out all by yourself. It's bad enough that you haven't been kissed; telling people about it will only make your life more difficult. You don't want anyone to laugh at you. If something like this gets around, you'll be the joke of the entire campus....*

Torn between two things and not wanting to choose either one, I bit my lower lip and hesitantly looked at my friends.

Then, in a final and mournful moment, I realized that the girls would figure out the basics of my secret even if I didn't tell them. Helpless to change that fact, I cleared my throat a few times and tried to smile. Licking my lips, I prepared to break the silence.

The topic had been bottled up inside of me for so long that my ability to speak momentarily failed; it was difficult to even know what I should say. My voice shook a little, and the words came out rather simply:

"Actually ... I'm still waiting for *my* first kiss."

The girls stared at me for a moment before they said anything, and I prepared myself for the absolute worst. It seemed as if it took ages, but eventually they spoke.

Their response shocked me.

This Is Romance?

My friends started talking in animated voices about how romantic it was that I had yet to experience a single smooch. I could hardly believe my ears. *Romantic?* I had certainly never used that term to describe my situation. Expressions like *horrific, ghastly,* and *hideous*—now, those words were familiar to me! With bright, dancing eyes, though, and wide smiles on their faces, my friends kept chattering.

When the excited buzz died down a little, one of the girls began to share some personal information of her own. As her fingers numbered them off, she mentioned each of the guys she had kissed in her lifetime. There were quite a few of them, and as she spoke I wondered exactly where she was going with her story. When the tally was finally over, she revealed the moral behind her tale.

"You know," she said, "I honestly wish I could have what you have, Lisa. After just so many kisses, you get to the point where kissing isn't even special anymore."

To my astonishment, the other girls agreed. My brain started to hurt.

When all of the first-kiss admissions were over, I retreated to my own room in a daze. I needed to figure some things out.

With all of my heart I wanted to believe the things that my friends were telling me. I wanted to think that my life was romantic, that I hadn't missed out on much, and that kisses could be something less than extraordinary. I wanted to believe that it was *I* who was the lucky one in the room—that inexperience in romance really *could* be good. But, you see, none of it seemed to be true.

I didn't feel lucky. I didn't see any romance in my life and I *had* missed out on things—a lot of things. I had missed out on school dances, shared umbrellas, and midnight kisses on New Year's Eve. I had missed out on valentines and late-night phone calls. I had missed out on winks, hugs, and heart-shaped picture frames.

From what I could tell, there had never been anything good about being single. In fact, my single status had always been the one thing in my life that I truly hated. But then, about an hour after shamefully admitting to having virgin lips, something began to change inside of me—ever so slightly.

As hard as I tried, I couldn't keep my mind from replaying the conversation that I had just had with my friends. Over and over I heard the same words in my head: *I wish I could have what you have, Lisa.... I wish I could have what you have....*

Regardless of all the things that I felt and all the things that I knew to be true, I couldn't help but wonder if there was some truth behind my friends' claims too. Surprisingly, I found a part of myself hoping that the girls *were* right. Hoping that the things I had always envied weren't quite as wonderful as they seemed. Hoping that the life I had lived and loathed for so long was really not that bad after all.

And so, in spite of myself, I began to doubt—just a little—some of my perceptions about being unattached and unkissed.

That was the beginning of it, the beginning of everything.

A Plan in Motion

Originally a First Kiss Party was just another one of my weird ideas, and I must admit, even *I* thought it sounded stupid. But then, to my surprise, I got attached to the notion, and I decided to go through with it—absurd as it may have seemed. I even got to the point where throwing my party seemed like a normal life event.

Not everyone agreed with that sentiment.

Take, for example, my parents. I was away at college, and the three of us were talking on the phone one day when I broke the news to them. Naturally, they thought it was a complete hoax, and they jokingly volunteered to buy the first supplies for my party.

A few weeks later I went home from school for a couple of days and asked my mom when she planned to go shopping for decorations. "You mean you weren't kidding about that?" she asked. One look at my sheepish expression told her that I was serious. In response, she rolled her eyes and laughed sympathetically, and I couldn't help but giggle right along with her.

Back at college the following week, I received a package from my family. At the very bottom of the parcel, among some homemade goodies and notes, I found a medium-sized gift bag, filled to the brim with party supplies. On the front of the colorful sack was a big red heart with a message in my mom's handwriting:

To Lisa
Love & Hugs, Mom and Dad.
Have a great time celebrating!

That gift bag from my parents was the perfect way for me to jump-start what has now become quite a ridiculous stockpile of stuff. Today, I have packets and packets of party supplies, including balloons, ribbons, noisemakers, streamers, hats, napkins, and confetti. All of them remain unopened in their original clear plastic wrap—waiting, just like me, for the big day. The day that I finally get kissed.

The Rest of the Story

With my closetful of party supplies, I'd love to be able to say that everything is perfect all the time now. I'd love to tell you that I don't mind being unkissed at all, that I don't care if guys ask me out or not, and that I don't struggle with the same old insecurities.

I can't say any of those things honestly. There are still days when I hate my virgin lips more than anything else. Even today I might feel a lump rising in my throat when the flowers get delivered to someone else. I still struggle to find confidence on lonely Friday nights.

I'm not sure if any of my self-esteem issues will ever go away completely. They might; they might not. What I *do* know, though, is that they have gotten better. Much better. Immeasurably better.

Planning a First Kiss Party has been a fun addition to my life, but it hasn't been the only thing that has changed for me over the last two years. In reality, the party itself is just the tip of my iceberg, because the biggest change that has happened to me has been a change *within*.

I used to think that a fairy tale relationship would fill the emptiness that I felt inside of me. I thought that if only a guy would accept and approve of me, somehow my life would seem less vacant. In my twisted view of the world, I was certain that dates and kisses would make me feel worthwhile, valuable, and whole.

I couldn't have been more wrong.

Today, rather than seeking satisfaction in a relationship that could fade, I'm learning how to fill my life with things that can bring true contentment—things that will last forever. Instead of defining myself by the number of boyfriends, dates, or kisses that I have had (or, haven't had), I'm finding that my *true* identity comes from being a daughter of God. Although it often seems impossible to move beyond "Never Been Kissed," I know that I must seek to do so. No matter how much my loneliness consumes me, I must strive to get past it. I must become more than my dating status.

It's so tempting for me to look in the mirror and to see there nothing more than a girl who can't get a date. When I evaluate my life, it's hard not to focus on the fact that I'm a perpetually single person who has gone two decades with virgin lips. It's tempting, it's hard, but I know that I am much more than those things.

I often let myself forget that God thinks I'm great enough to deserve His love—the best love the universe has to offer. He loves me enough to sacrifice His Son for me. I often forget that He cares about me that much. His opinion of me doesn't even factor in my dating status.

I'm working hard at trying to see myself the way that God sees me, trying to look at the world through His eyes. The better I get at viewing love and romance from God's point of view, the less trouble I have accepting my own love story—or complete lack thereof.

So today, although my dating status has not changed in the least, I know true happiness. Despite my inexperience in romance, life doesn't seem empty anymore. And even though I'm still waiting to be kissed, I understand what it is to feel like a treasure.

Now, take it from a girl who really knows her party stuff: more than anything, those things are worth celebrating.

TWO

GREAT WHITE SPACES

"For I know the plans I have for you," declares the Lord.

JEREMIAH 29:11a

Kelly Moore, bless her heart, was eight years older than I. She was kind and pretty, she had great fashion sense, and she drove a cool car. What's more, she was a *high school graduate*, and she worked at a local beauty salon, which meant that she knew how to create all of the best-looking hairstyles. Naturally, I idolized her, and I thought that we should be best friends.

One summer Kelly was a counselor at my church's youth camp, and when I found out that she bunked in the cabin next to mine, I got so excited that I could hardly function. I became obsessed, making sure I knew exactly where Kelly would be at all times. I turned into her second shadow, laughing too much at all of her jokes, watching her eat breakfast, lunch, and dinner, and absorbing everything she said like an annoying little sponge.

After a couple hours of blatant worship, I decided that I knew Kelly well enough to start prying into her life. I began by asking her some simple questions about her job, her family, and her friends. After covering those basics, I awkwardly switched topics to the one thing that I really wanted to discuss: Kelly's love life.

Being the nosy little leech that I was, I already knew that Kelly wasn't in a dating relationship. But I wanted to know *details.* I asked her how long it had been since she'd been out on a date, who her last boyfriend was, and which guy she was currently interested in. I wanted to know what her "type" was, which male counselor was her favorite, and what eye color she liked best on guys. I pried like no self-respecting twelve-year-old ever should; I even offered to set her up with our church's cute summer intern.

Kelly looked a little dazed at my barrage of curiosity, but she did her best to answer my questions. I listened with awe and wonder, especially when she got to the juicy parts. She said that she thought some of the camp counselors were cute, and some of them even seemed to be her type!

But then, in the last few moments of our little chat, Kelly took the conversation for an unexpected turn. I could hardly believe what she said. "Honestly," she told me, "I feel really content being single right now, and I'm not looking for anyone in particular."

What?

I was dumbfounded. *Content?* Content *and* single? I didn't think that the two things could happen at the same time.

Impossibilities

Now, Kelly was not the first person who had ever stunned me with such a claim. I had previously met quite a few other women who had declared that they were satisfied without romance. And although it had never seemed as if they were lying to me, I didn't ever get to the point where I could actually believe them. No matter how wonderful they said their lives were, I couldn't imagine a woman feeling true happiness unless a guy's fingers were interlocking with hers.

Even as a sixth grader, you see, I knew that there was just something special about romance. The tiniest sliver of it could give me wings. There was no feeling like being tongue-tied, flustered, nervous, and excited all at the same time. I loved it when a giddy smile invaded my face and when I couldn't keep my eyes from sparkling.

From my point of view, the only things that could make me feel better than a guy's smile were a guy's hug and a guy's wink. I didn't understand how life could feel complete without such things. It just didn't seem possible.

Still, as skeptical as I was toward "content women" like Kelly, there was something about them that I couldn't keep myself from admiring. They seemed peaceful and relaxed in their approach to life and love, and their calm sense of trust demanded my respect. As my admiration for such women grew, I began to wonder if they saw something that I didn't.

Could it be possible to be satisfied without romance? I often wondered. According to women like Kelly, it certainly was. But everything I had ever known made me think the exact opposite.

Damsel in Distress

Like many young women today, I grew up on a generous diet of fairy tales. Reading through my storybooks, I learned about talking mirrors, magnificent castles, glass slippers, and mining dwarves. More than anything, though, I learned about princes.

As I easily discovered, a prince was the answer to all of life's problems. Not only could he waltz me around in his father's ballroom, but he could rescue me from a forbidding tower, a poisonous apple, or a life of servitude. All he needed was a white horse and an enchanted pair of lips.

Now, I knew that fairy tales weren't true. I knew that they were stories with invented people and invented places and invented ideas. Even so, I felt that I understood many of their characters. I could easily relate to Cinderella, Sleeping Beauty, and Snow White. I too was waiting for my prince.

At an early age I had begun dreaming that an amazing guy (shining armor optional, of course) would come along for me someday. *If only that would happen,* I thought, *everything would turn out all right.* My sky would be forever blue. The negative feelings inside of me would fade away, and I wouldn't be lonely anymore. With his hand in mine, I would feel beautiful. And, surely, if he would just kiss me, life would be glorious.

So day after day I dreamed about the time when my prince would finally find me. I pictured my future in the arms of my ideal guy, and I really liked the things I saw in that fantasy world. So I allowed myself to dream much and to dream often.

What I didn't realize was that I was dreaming with the wrong perspective.

Avoiding Purple Zebras

"Why are you guys way back here?" I asked my friend Monica.

She gave me a *look* and didn't say anything. Confused, I laid down my hammer and followed Monica's line of vision to the mural she was working on.

I was seventeen years old, and I was participating in a work project to help "spruce up" a mountain church in South America. Because this particular church did a lot of outreach for underprivileged children in the area, one of our assignments was to paint an outdoor mural showing the story of Noah's Ark. Since I'm not exactly a painter, I stuck to the other jobs on our worksite—things like cement-mixing and bricklaying. Occasionally, though, when I needed a break from my shovel and my work gloves, I would stop by the artistic group to check out their progress.

On almost all of my visits to the mural site, I was greeted by a mass of hands and arms fluttering away. After only a few hours on task, the project had begun to take shape. What started out as a dirty brick wall soon became a grid of pencil lines, the pattern for a cartoon Noah and his cartoon boat. Later the huge white space was splattered with tiger stripes and alligator scales. Then flying brushes added more colors, each hand seemingly trying to beat all of the others at emptying his or her little colored palette.

On this particular lunch break, though, as I walked by the mural site, no one was painting. The work was nowhere near done, but all of the artists had stepped back about twenty feet from Noah and his ark.

"Why are you guys way back here?" I asked again. "Why

aren't you working?"

"We *are* working," Monica told me with an exasperated sigh and another *look*.

Hmm, right, I thought, and I picked up my hammer.

Later Monica explained what had happened. Right before I had approached the artists, she told me, someone had made a mistake on the mural—a big mistake. The person had completely painted over a boundary line, and as a result, an entire section of Noah's ark had been painted the wrong color.

"*That* is why we were all looking at the mural," Monica said simply.

I didn't understand. What did *looking* have to do with the problem? *Looking* didn't fix anything.

Monica noticed my confused expression and gave me a generous smile. Then she proceeded to give me a helpful lesson in art.

On a large project, she told me (like, say, a mural), an artist should never spend too much time looking at small sections of the work. If a painter were to keep his nose right up next to Noah the whole time, he would lose sight of the rest of the painting. In doing so, he would be much more likely to make an incorrect brushstroke or to use the wrong color on something. For example, he might unintentionally paint a zebra purple or make a polar bear blue. He might completely paint over a line, only to have to go back and redo it later.

In mural painting, I learned, a too-narrow perspective will often cause big problems. And as I found out later, so it is with everything else.

Nose to the Wall

Life as a young woman often feels a lot like watching someone paint a mural. You stand back, arms crossed in front of your chest, and you observe as the Master Painter and Designer fills in the white spaces of your existence.

During childhood He paints things like "learning how to read," "playtime," and "naps" into the picture. A few years later you watch as He adds things like "school," "mischief," and "slumber parties" to the mix. Over time your colors start to blend together, and the beginnings of a true work of art can be seen.

But then, in the midst of the work, something catches your eye. In the top corner of the mural of your life you notice a white space—a glaringly empty white space.

Troubled, you approach the painting and begin to inspect the area. Then, with a look of confusion, you turn to the Artist.

"Lord, why isn't anything there yet?" you ask.

He keeps on painting.

You keep looking at the white space. "Lord, over here!" you say. "Wouldn't it be fun to paint this part?"

He keeps working, unmoved.

The white space glares more than ever, and you begin to get upset. "Lord, I would *really like it* if you could start painting some of this," you say.

He doesn't seem to hear you.

You try a different approach. "Lord, please?"

Still no response.

You turn back to the mural, hiding the look of disappointment on your face. *Why won't He get rid of this?* you wonder.

Doesn't He hear me? Surely He wouldn't ignore me, would He? After all, doesn't He want me to be happy?

Day after day the Artist works on your mural, but He never once lifts His paintbrush to the top corner—not even anywhere close to it. And you stop asking Him to. Instead you stare at your own emptiness, each day feeling more and more frustrated.

More and more angry.

More and more cheated.

More and more alone.

Your eyes fix on the top corner until they can't blur anymore. Then, with tears welling up and with a heart that hurts, you cry out, demanding an answer from the Artist.

"Lord, *can't you see all of this white space?*"

Slowly, deliberately, He keeps on painting.

Fill-Ups

I spent a large portion of my life staring at the top corner of my mural, and I spent a lot of my life getting angry at the Artist because He wasn't painting anything there. Like many of you, perhaps, I became frustrated and upset because there wasn't any romance to color my life. And over and over I asked my Creator to paint something—*anything*—in my "love" spot.

What I failed to recognize back then was that I had all but put my nose up against that corner of my mural. I had stopped looking at anything else in my life; all I did was wait for romance. And the longer I waited, the more intently I focused on my glaring white space.

For years I let a lack of romance dominate my field of vision. And when I say "years," I'm not kidding. From sixth grade all the way up until college, I was consumed by my single status.

But then I began planning a First Kiss Party. And oddly enough, *that* was what it took to help get the ball rolling.

It surprised me to discover that stocking up on party supplies was an absolute riot. (I'm very easily amused—can you tell?) Almost every weekend I made a trip to a store near my home and picked up something for my little celebration. On three consecutive Saturdays I bought packets of confetti pieces that were shaped like little lips.

Sometimes I would go to a store just to scout out its new stock. I would walk up and down the aisles, making mental notes of what types of balloons they carried and which color schemes looked best together.

The clerks at the stores probably thought I was psycho, but I didn't mind at all how crazy the whole thing seemed. I was having the time of my life. My First Kiss Party was an exciting new thrill for me, and it made things seem fresh and breezy. It was really, really *fun.*

And then, somehow, it became more than just fun.

A Step Back

Without ever actually intending to, I was taking some little steps away from the romance craze that I had been on for so long. Instead of focusing only on my lack of a love life, I had started concentrating on things like streamers and noisemakers.

Rather than searching town for a guy who would ask me out, I found myself scouring the sale racks for extra large balloons. For the first time in my life *I* had something that all those other girls didn't have; and for the first time in my life, I began to see a bigger picture.

I discovered that my life could be really fun, despite the fact that I didn't have a significant other. I found that there were things that *I* could do that girls who were dating couldn't do nearly as easily. And to top it all off, there were things about being "unkissed" that (in a weird and twisted way, of course) were really cool.

I can see now that many of the strengths in my life have come not *in spite* of singleness but *because* of it. *Because* I haven't dated anyone, I have been able to learn tons of important lessons—lessons that will be huge helps to me if I ever do start dating. *Because* I haven't been asked out, I have learned how to be a better friend, how to depend on God for my self-esteem, and how to better live in purity. And as much as I hate to admit it, *because* I haven't been kissed, I have developed a better understanding of regret, patience, and purity.

Now, I haven't sought to completely ignore the white space in my life. I can't. It's a big part of my mural, after all.

Thinking about romance still has a way of turning everything into hearts and stars and smiles and roses. Weddings still make me all warm inside, and I still practically fall over when a guy sings a love song *a cappella*. I still love it when my heart gets fluttery inside or when my stomach experiences a sudden drop in altitude. My movie drawer is still stocked with all the classic "chick flicks." But today, rather than making it my whole picture, I've made romance just a *part* of my life.

If only I would have stepped back earlier, I would have been able to see past my white space. If only I would have stopped focusing on romance so much, I would have been able to see the rest of my mural. And I would have seen that God was already putting beauty into my life. He was just painting in other areas.

On the Way

One of the things that helped me along in this process was some biblical insight that my friend Darren found in the Book of Acts. The story opens in the early years of Christianity, when there were explosive things going on in churches all over the Middle East and in Europe. One such place is where we find a man named Philip, our main character.

Philip lived in the central area of Israel, a place called Samaria. He was deeply involved in a fledgling Christian community there, and he had been a part of exciting happenings in its church. After a time, though, he felt that God was calling him to a different place.

Philip followed God's lead, leaving Samaria and heading down the road to a place called Capernaum. While he was traveling, he came across an Ethiopian eunuch who had a few questions about some of the books of the Bible. Philip stopped, took the time to answer the man's questions, and then went on to tell him about Jesus Christ and the salvation that God offered.

The eunuch was so excited to hear this news that he accepted God's salvation and was baptized on the spot. He eventually went home to Ethiopia, and scholars today wonder if he was the man who first brought Christianity to the continent of Africa.

But let's get back to our main character. On his way to Capernaum, Philip had a lot of things to think about, a lot of things to prepare for. He probably never expected such an important ministry to happen when he was in between two other ones. He could have kept his focus on the place where he was going, eyes fixed on the road ahead. He stopped, though, and found that sometimes the most amazing things happen *on the way*.

Sometimes it may feel like singleness is nothing more than a lonely, empty road between playground kisses and wedding bells. When traveling such a road, it's really easy to become consumed by our circumstances and frustrated by our lack of love. All the while, though, we pass up countless opportunities to make a difference at the roadside. If only, like Philip, we can learn to take our eyes off the next bustling metropolis for a moment, we will find that God has great things to offer us right now.

Although this road seems long, dusty, and very lonely at times, even here it is often the most amazing things that happen *on the way*.

The New Perspective

Possibly more than anything else, longing for romance can make us lose sight of opportunities at the roadside. Because the idea of having a significant other is so exciting to us, it's easy to let romance be the only thing we look for in life.

We rush to our mural, keeping at least one eye fixed on the top corner, waiting for our white spaces to be filled up. After a time, if nothing appears there, we walk right up to the mural, tapping our feet and clearing our throats. Hoping to make the Artist change the order of His design. Hoping that He will come and fill the white space.

But when we step back and begin to see the big picture, everything changes. We start to see color in other areas. As we become less focused on romance, we are able to watch as God fills different places of our lives. And we find that, as one book says, "there *is* more God has for us during a season of single-ness than just learning the art of misery and impatience."[1]

Do you ever find yourself disagreeing with such a statement? Do you ever find yourself staring at a big, glaring white space? Do you find it hard to see beauty in your own life? Do you ever get the feeling that there might be something that you're missing? If so, will you take a few steps back with me?

Will you?

Come on. God is still painting, and He's working on a masterpiece.

THREE

A NOT-SO LEAP OF FAITH

I wait for the Lord, my soul waits, and in his word I put my hope.

PSALM 130:5

When I was four or five years old my family went over to some relatives' house on a hot summer day so we could play in their pool. At the time I couldn't swim worth two hoots, but I certainly didn't want to be left out of all the family fun. So to help me out, my dad arranged a nice little system for the two of us.

I would stand on the edge of the deck near the pool, and he would get into the water and walk over to where I was standing. As soon as he got there, I would spring myself off the deck, hands flailing, legs kicking, little chubby tummy first. Then I would land with a splash into his outstretched arms.

I absolutely *loved* this little system, and as our day in the sun wore on, I made my dad catch me over and over and over again. No sooner would he place me on the deck than I was ready to jump again. I barely gave my bathing suit a chance to drip. I was having so much fun that I just couldn't get enough.

But then, right in the middle of our game, something

happened. Another person in the pool came over to our corner and started a conversation with my dad. My father, being the nice guy that he is, paused from his catching and turned to chat for a minute or two.

My fun stopped.

There I stood on the deck, two dripping ponytails and one huge attitude. (You know what they say about redheads and tempers. Well, let's just say that it's all true.) With my hands on my hips, I glared at my dad and fumed inside: *Hello, I'm waiting here....*

He hardly paid me any attention, and he certainly didn't put his arms out so I could jump again.

That was it. I had had *enough.* With a huge swing of my arms, I launched myself off the deck.

On the Loose

To this day I can recall what the next few moments felt like. As soon as I reached midair, I panicked. Time seemed to stop, and I couldn't remember how logic had brought me to my airborne state. All I could think of was that I did *not* want to land in the pool anymore. A second later, though, that fear submerged into reality as my little body plunged below the surface.

I had never been completely under water all by myself, and I can't think of another time when I felt so helpless. I couldn't swim, I couldn't float, I couldn't scream. I didn't even know that I was supposed to hold my breath under water.

In the midst of my terror, though, what I didn't know was that my dad had seen me hit the water. I was only in the pool for a second or two before he plucked me out and lifted me back onto the deck. Then, as I sat half-whimpering and half-coughing at the water's edge, my dad gave me a hug and took some time to explain the importance of patience.

Fifteen years later, it's amazing to think that I'm still trying to learn that same lesson.

Splish, Splash

It seems that it has always been instinctive for me to be a *jumper.* No matter the time or place or circumstance, it has been built into my nature to want to flee whatever pool deck I find myself on.

When I was little, my mom would always say, "Patience is a virtue, Lisa." When I got older and sassy, I would respond to that statement with, "Yeah, but it's a virtue that I don't have."

I hate feeling delayed, and I'll avoid waiting at almost any cost. When I'm at the grocery store, I always try to pick the shortest line and the fastest checkout clerk. While I'm driving, I weave in and out of traffic, searching for the fastest lane. Yield signs make me fidgety. I flip back and forth between TV channels on commercial breaks. I don't like it when people walk slowly, talk slowly, chew slowly, or work slowly.

Whenever I *have* to wait for something, my default mode is most certainly *not* patience. Like a hasty little five-year-old, I squint my eyes, set my jaw, and sigh—loudly. If that doesn't do the trick, I tap my foot and put my hands on my hips—indignant that I have been left to drip outside the pool.

It should come as no surprise, then, that one of the things

I find most frustrating about being single is that it requires a certain amount of waiting. OK, a *lot* of waiting.

Not only do I have to wait until I find a guy, but I have to wait until I find one I like. (This is much harder than it may initially sound, because I'm choosing from a supply that seems pretty meager at times.) Assuming that I happen to be fortunate enough to locate a guy who fits my criteria, the waiting has only just begun. Next I must wait for him to notice me— which usually takes at least a year or so. Then, if the two of us finally do reach a first-name-and-waving basis, I have to wait and see if the proverbial sparks ever begin to fly.

After only so much hanging around, a girl starts to go crazy. And so, instead of waiting, I jump. And I expect things to be ready for me the moment I hit the water.

Up in the Air

"That's it!" said Natalie. "I'm telling him."

"No!" I responded, my eyes wide and my voice intense. "You just can't."

"Oh, yes, I can," she snapped back at me. "You said I could."

"Well...," I stammered, tripping over my tongue, "I changed my mind."

"I don't care," she said. "I am sick of your changing your mind. I'm telling him."

I didn't know if I should smile at her or glare at her.

"You know that you want Eric to know that you like him," Natalie said, her eyebrows rising and her mouth curling at the edges. "You *know* you do."

I had to pinch my lips together to keep a smile under control. My eyes were twinkling like a thousand stars. "Yeah, I guess I do," I said quietly.

"YES!" she gushed, running for the door. "And now I'm leaving before you have time to change your mind again."

As my friend fled the room, I laughed and yelled a final warning at her back. "Fine, Natalie, you can tell him whatever you want! But you better not make it sound like I'm desperate!"

Before I even finished hollering the words, she was gone. Then, in the privacy of my empty room, I let out a nervous giggle and tried to decide if I really *did* want him to know.

Moving Day

With romantic relationships, it seems like it is particularly easy to launch ourselves off the pool deck. The water looks so warm and inviting, so clear, so refreshing, so perfect and wonderful.

Especially when you're not in it.

I could have waited around to see if Eric would ever notice me. I could have let him initiate something. I could have endured a few more days of strategically sitting two tables away from his usual spot in the lunchroom.

I could have waited, but I didn't want to. I was sick of twiddling my thumbs and smiling contentedly whenever he was around. I was sick of letting our conversations end with a friendly "Good night" or "See ya later." I was sick of watching him talk to other girls and having to wonder about how I compared to them. I was sick of acting casual—as if my heart didn't race every time he came within a hundred feet of me. I was sick of waiting to see if he would make a move.

And so *I* moved. At least I started to.

Take a Number

I have often thought that being single is a whole lot like being in the waiting room at a doctor's office. Your eyes glaze over as you sit in a chair on wheels and stare at the fake tree in the corner. (You can always tell that the tree is fake because it has been "planted" in that stringy craft-store moss instead of dirt.) Elsewhere around the waiting room are enormous plaques of wood and brass that proudly display the resident doctor's credentials. A little area is filled with toys and crayons, and there is a stack of outdated magazines on the coffee table.

But the most noticeable feature in the room is a slowly ticking clock that has been prominently hung on the wall directly in front of you. Loudly, continually, it reminds you of how long you've been sitting there.

Tick-tock, tick-tock.

Waiting for romance feels like sitting in a physician's waiting room, right down to the fake tree in the corner. As time passes by, it is here where we must sit and wonder if the Love Doctor will ever call our names. This is the place where we take a number, waiting to see if dreams of romance will ever come true.

For some individuals, this waiting room experience is a short one; it seems as if their names have been called before they even set foot on the premises. (These are the people whom everyone else wants to dislike.) Others have just enough time to announce their arrival and be seated, and then they are hastily escorted to a back room.

And then there are others of us who wait. And then, maybe, we wait a bit more. Some of us wait so long that we're pretty sure our backsides have made permanent impressions in our chairs.

It's no surprise that another term for "patient" is "long-suffering." I often feel like *suffer* is the perfect word to describe my situation.

A Striped Shirt

Honestly, how in the world is a girl supposed to be patient in matters of guys and romance? Just about any kind of waiting can be frustrating, but when you throw words like "love of a lifetime" and "soul mate" into the mix, patience can seem almost impossible.

If there's anything that can make me want to *jump* in life, it's the prospect of romance on my horizon. (You know—that elated feeling you get when a guy remembers your name after only three to five introductions.) Before I even have a chance to think, my adrenaline surges, and I'm ready to vault myself—headfirst and heart-first—right off of the Singles Deck.

Here's a perfect example: My sophomore year in college, a guy in one of my literature classes caught my eye. Shortly after this I was having dinner with my friend Josh in the school cafeteria. (I should note here that Josh gets a huge thrill out of other people's embarrassment.)

As Josh and I were eating, I spotted my Literature Guy across the room, and (of course) that whole adrenaline thing happened. So, in a classic example of my *jumping* tendency, I pointed out to Josh the "so cute" Literature Guy. I even commented on how nice he looked in his blue-and-white-striped shirt. Josh turned around to see, raised an eyebrow, and said nothing.

Ten minutes later Josh and I had finished eating, so we got up to return our dinner trays to the kitchen. Josh was walking about fifteen feet in front of me, when suddenly he stopped and turned around. Then, pointing to his right—pointing *directly at my Literature Guy*—he yelled back at me, "HEY, LISA, ISN'T THAT THE GUY YOU THINK IS CUTE?"

My mouth dropped open, and my face turned six shades of red. Two thoughts rushed through my head: *Oh, no!* and *Must get out of here!* I quickened my pace and breezed past Josh, gluing my eyes to the floor and hoping that the humiliation was over.

It wasn't.

"HEY, LISA, ISN'T THAT HIM?" Josh yelled. "THE ONE SITTING RIGHT OVER THERE IN THE BLUE-AND-WHITE-STRIPED SHIRT?"

Six more shades of red were added to my face. I popped my dinner tray on a conveyor belt, spun myself around, and bolted for the door. On my way out I saw Josh's evil little smile, and I heard bellows of laughter coming from the thirty or so guys who surrounded that one blue-and-white shirt.

I can't say that I didn't have it coming. I knew about Josh's teasing nature long before he revealed my crush to the school cafeteria. In fact, that teasing nature was the main reason why

I had told him about my crush in the first place.

As far as relationships go, my primary method of jumping almost always involves a person like Josh—a friend who either really likes teasing me or who can't keep his mouth shut. (In Josh's case, it was the former.) Over the years I've relied on quite a few "Joshes" to help me out.

Here's how it normally works: I set my sights on a certain guy in my life and decide that he should ask me out. Soon. Then I do my best to smile and giggle and toss my hair whenever he's around, hoping that he'll get the picture and come ask for my number. When that doesn't work, I introduce myself a few times. When that doesn't work, I get sick of waiting. I get tired of patience, and I jump. I go find myself a Josh.

"Joshes" are people whom I use to manipulate my situation so I can get a date. I tell them about my particular crush with the hope that they will tell the guy that I like him—either by teasing or by blabbing. This will (I convince myself) inspire the guy to notice me more and to fall head-over-heels for me. *If Josh does his job properly,* I think, *I'll get what I want precisely when I want it.*

Why, When, Why Not?

It's crazy. Every time I jump, I start to see a bigger picture the minute I reach midair. But then, of course, it's already too late.

The Literature Guy saga is not the only one of its kind in the story of my life. There are many others, to be sure. Out of all of them, though, I cannot think of a single time that I have jumped prematurely without regretting it. I can't think of one significant moment when my impatience has ever done me much good.

But, oh, how I must continually fight against my urge to jump.

I'm convinced that every girl has her own breaking point—that place where she stops waiting and starts manipulating. She stops trusting and she starts trying. Dissatisfied with her situation, she waves God away, saying, "Thanks, Lord, but I can take it from here." Then she jumps.

As Oswald Chambers writes, "One of the greatest strains in life is the strain of waiting for God."[1] That's so true, isn't it? We struggle endlessly to learn patience for God's timing of things.

Lord, why won't You let me fall in love today?

Lord, why don't I have any romance in my life at this instant?

Lord, why can't I meet my husband right now?

Lord, if it's not gonna happen today, can You at least tell me when it will?

And so the saga continues.

I know how frustrating it can be when your Literature Guy doesn't call or when he doesn't catch on to your shy smiles. I know that it stinks when he picks someone else, and I understand how it makes your heart ache when there is no *him* in sight. I really *do* know how hard it is to wait for romance and Prince Charming. Trust me—I'm living it too.

But for the sake of our collective sanity, can we try (just for a minute or two) to put all of those things aside?

Come with me. Let's take a few steps back and try to look at patience with a "big picture" mentality.

An Old, Old Song

Song of Songs is a book in the Old Testament that focuses specifically on love. Despite what its title might imply, this book does not come in the form of sheet music. Rather, it is a short poetic work—only eight chapters—that details the romantic love of a man and a woman. I especially like what my NIV Study Bible has to say about this book: "In the Song,... love ... finds words."[2]

So what exactly does this Song have to say about love? Well, it says a whole lot of things, but we'll just look at one here. (You can read the rest for yourself!)

Repeatedly in Song of Songs this phrase appears: *Do not arouse or awaken love until it so desires.*[3]

That's scary, isn't it? (If you're anything like me, you probably just recoiled at the very thought.)

I don't like to be reminded that I'm supposed to be patient. I especially don't like to be reminded that I'm supposed to be patient in matters of love. However, the more I observe coed relationships, the more I begin to believe that (just maybe) patience is really the best way to go. For us women, that is.

You've probably noticed that many of the times a female initiates romance in a relationship, the connection doesn't end up faring well for her. After a date or two or three, the excitement fizzles, and the relationship ends. Why? Well, as much as I hate reducing things to X and Y chromosomes, it's impossible to ignore the fact that there are huge differences between the way guys approach romance and the way girls do.

As a general rule, females seem to suffer from what has been described as K.I.S.A.S. (Knight In Shining Armor

Syndrome, for those of you who are wondering). Deep down, most of us want to find a man who would be willing to fight for us (as long as nobody gets hurt, of course). We long for the day when a prince will come along to rescue us, and we really like the idea of riding off into a pink sunset.

Now, as far as guys go, what can I say? They're crazy. They're immature. But they're *cute* too, so I'll continue.

The Two Cs

If you were to observe a group of average teen or young adult males, you'd quickly find that they still display many of the qualities that they had in elementary school. You know: beating each other up, grossing girls out, making disgusting noises at the table, and that kind of stuff. But far above all those things, there are two inherently masculine characteristics that stand out. They are the "Two Cs":

C#1: *Challenge.* (They love it.)
C#2: *Competition.* (They can't get enough.)

Now, when I say this, I'm not saying that competitive women are manly women, and I'm not saying that women can't enjoy a good challenge. No, no, no. I consider myself to be a very competitive and challenge-loving person, and I have no problems with that. What I *am* saying is that guys tend to thrive on these things much more than girls do.

Guys love fixing things that are broken, lifting things that are heavy, and opening stubborn pickle jars. They love to conquer a challenge.

Guys love running faster than the high school track star, throwing farther than the starting quarterback, and having a shinier car than the guy next door. They love to beat their competition.

In the same way that the "Two Cs" affect the sports, weights, and vehicles in a young man's life, they also affect his relationships with girls. Most guys prefer to date girls who will present them with a "challenge" of sorts, and most guys like to feel that they've "competed" for a girl. As the poet George Meredith wrote over a century ago, "She whom I love is hard to catch and conquer, Hard, but O the glory of the winning were she won."[4]

The great thing about K.I.S.A.S. and the Two Cs is that they usually complement each other very well. Girls get to be rescued, and guys get to be challenged and victorious. However, when impatience is added to Knight In Shining Armor Syndrome, things quickly begin to go awry.

When a girl's impatience gets the best of her, she usually ends up taking the first steps toward romance in a relationship. Because she wants so badly to find her royal knight, she'll call a guy and ask him out, she'll give a guy her number and "suggest" that he call her, or she'll have a friend tell him that she's interested. (Hmm ... sounds familiar.)

While all of these things may seem completely innocent, they are very damaging to any possibility of a lasting romance. Here's why: When a girl gives a guy 100 percent assurance that she'll go out with him if he asks, she effectively eliminates both of the "Cs" that he wants to have. The challenge is gone, because he already knows what the outcome of an invitation will be. Not only that, but all of his competition has been obliterated. He knows that she wants *him*.

A relationship that might have had real potential for excitement suddenly becomes very boring. A girl who might have been at the top of his list suddenly becomes run-of-the-mill. The adventure of pursuit and the thrill of rivalry are gone—all because the girl wouldn't let him chase her.

A Prayer in the Margin

So it seems that the Book of Proverbs is still right: "A patient man [or woman] has great understanding."[5] As difficult as it is for us to wait for romance and as difficult as it is to avoid jumping, we really are better off that way.

That doesn't make it any easier, though, does it?

The tough thing about patience is that it asks a lot of us. For one, it requires huge amounts of faith and trust. In order to wait for romance in my life, I must be able to believe that God's timing of events is what's best for me. I have to trust that He'll work out the events of my life in the right sequence and on a perfect schedule. Not only that, but I must also surrender my will to His, believing that He'll bring me a boyfriend if I need one—that He'll give me a love story if I need one.

By no means are these low expectations.

I would be the first to tell you that patience is not easy. Some of my biggest cry fests have stemmed from the fear that I'll never experience love. Some of my very worst red-faced and downright puffy-eyed (not to mention runny-nosed) weep sessions have occurred because I'm scared that God's plans for romance are different from my own.

A few years ago, on a particularly difficult day, I opened my

Bible to Song of Songs and reread the Old Testament love story. Then, when I was finished, I handwrote a little prayer in the margin—right next to one of those "Do not arouse or awaken" verses. You might be able to relate to this prayer, so I'll give you a peek at it. It's dated November 1 of the year 2000, and this is what it says:

> Lord, give me the patience to wait for a man whom You may or may not give me. Help me to wait on You and on Your timing. I know that Your plan is best, but sometimes I just don't feel it in my heart. Remind me of Your love. Be my first love forever.
>
> ~Lisa

Praying such a prayer is easier on some days than it is on others. There are still times when I have to fight to keep from jumping, and there are still days when I get frustrated by all of this waiting. But I can tell you this: On the most difficult of days, God's touch is the most tender of all. In the moments that I feel completely alone and unlovable, He meets me at my bedside and traces the tears as they fall.

And then, through all of the junk and all of the struggle, waiting does begin to feel more comfortable. The urge to jump does get weaker. And with each of these developments, life as a single woman seems a bit more bearable, a bit improved.

Are you willing to test this waiting thing with me? Are you willing to work on your patience?

Let's try to practice *not* jumping for a while. In the words of Psalm 27, let's "wait for the Lord; be strong and take heart and wait for the Lord."[6] Let's trust that God's Word is right on this subject, and let's learn to stand on the deck for a while—dripping if we have to.

The pool will still be there when He's ready for us.

On Deck

I was almost prepared to put the phone down, but Natalie picked up just before her answering machine came on.

"Hi, Natalie, it's me," I said quickly, trying not to lose my cool.

"Hey, Lisa. What's up?"

"Um," I started, "I wanted to talk to you about this whole 'Eric' thing."

"OK," she said slowly, "what about it?"

Here goes, I thought.

"Well," I said, "I've decided that I *don't* want him to know that I like him."

"All right," she responded with a laugh.

"No, I'm really serious this time," I told her. (My tone was serious, too.) "I don't even want him to know that I think he's cute. And I don't care how many times you and I talk about it, I don't ever want you to let me let you let him know."

"OK," said Natalie (she knows me so well!). "It's a deal."

"Thanks," I said.

Natalie and I exchanged goodbyes, and I hung up my phone with a sigh.

Months later Eric still hasn't called me. We're still nothing more than friends—and I'm even beginning to believe that we're better off this way. But regardless of what happens with him, our story has a happy ending—a happy *un*ending:

I never jumped.

FOUR

NO MORE CHEESE, PLEASE

He heals the brokenhearted and binds up their wounds.
PSALM 147:3

Should I wear the white sweater or the black one?"
Samantha asked me.

I cocked my head to one side and tried to figure out which top would look best for a first date.

"Well," I said, "the white one's a little warmer, so you wouldn't have to wear a coat with that one."

"True," she said, squinting at the mirror. "I just don't know, though. I want to look nice, but I don't want to look like I'm trying too hard. We're going to be outside, after all."

Samantha tried on the black sweater one more time before deciding to go with the white one. Then, with a final spritz of perfume and a reapplication of her lipstick, she was ready to go—a half hour early, of course.

For the next twenty-five minutes Samantha tried to busy herself around the house. "I'm just trying not to get nervous," she explained. She straightened the pillows on her bed, moved some stuff around on her dresser, and tried to read a magazine.

But then, five minutes before her date was scheduled to show up, her excitement got the best of her. She bounced around the room, her mouth going back and forth between a nervous grin and a beaming smile. She stood in front of the mirror a few more times, quickly shifting her balance from left to right.

At last she couldn't take it any longer. "When is he going to *get* here?" she spurted out.

Minutes later Mark showed up at the door. He rattled off a practiced greeting, she blushed and giggled, and they walked out together.

For the next few weeks Samantha's days were filled with flirtatious instant messages and unexpected flowers. Then came late-night phone calls and walks in the park. She practically floated through the dates on her calendar, smiling the whole time. It felt good to be starting a relationship.

As she got to know Mark better, though, Samantha started getting the impression that he wasn't the right kind of guy for her. In the midst of all her elation, she noticed some inconsistencies in his spiritual life, and she could see that his personality didn't work very well with hers.

Samantha was torn. She knew that her relationship with Mark wasn't the best thing for her, but she didn't want to let go of all the excitement it had brought into her life. She *liked* having bouquets of daisies sent to her. She *liked* having little cards appear in her mailbox. She *liked* being told that she was beautiful.

After praying for a week about her situation, Samantha knew what she needed to do. She got together with Mark and told him that she couldn't go out with him anymore. He agreed, and they broke things off.

I found out shortly after, when I asked Samantha how she was doing.

"Well," she said quietly, "Mark and I decided not to date anymore."

"Oh," I said. "And you're OK with that?"

Samantha sighed slowly and looked at the floor. "I'm OK with it. I mean, I know he's not the one for me or anything like that." Then, after a pause, she looked up and said, "It's just going to be really hard for me, not to be falling for someone."

A Tale As Old As Time

There seems to be a special part of women that responds with a lurch whenever we get extra doses of male attention. A cute little wave from a guy can easily make us overlook the fact that our jeans feel tight or that our hair is a disaster area. When he stops just to talk to us, we forget that we woke up feeling ugly.

Even the smallest hint of romance can make a girl feel great inside, can't it? With each glance out of the corner of a young man's eye, we feel valuable and esteemed. Even an awkward conversation with the guy next door can inspire a new freshness in us. If he winks, we're mush.

Even if we dislike a guy, we might still want him to be crazy about us. No matter how loud his chewing is or how ridiculous his attempts at facial hair, if he sends a special grin our way, we can get all jittery and pathetic inside. Deep down we'd like to think that every guy on the planet would fall all over himself for us if he had the opportunity.

Of course, things are even better when we meet someone great. It's crazy, isn't it? After hanging out with someone only a few times, we realize that we feel ten times better about ourselves whenever he's around. To quote a great movie line, "You know how it is. You're out with a guy and you find him attractive, and then suddenly everything they say sounds brilliant."

If they say we're nice, we'll believe it. If they say we're beautiful, we'll believe it. If they say we're Superwoman, we'll start stocking up on blue tights.

When we're feeling lonely or rejected or just plain low, it's easy for us to think that a romantic relationship is what we *really* need to feel better. After all, romance is what puts flowers in that empty vase in the cupboard. Romance is what brings gourmet chocolates to our door. Romance is what rescues us from our loneliness.

If only that smart guy from chemistry class would come our way, things would go better for us. If only the telephone call would be from that cute baseball player, we'd feel OK about ourselves. If only that guy down the street would stop by, life would be grand.

Wouldn't it?

Round One

When I was in elementary school, The Farmer in the Dell was my least favorite game to play. I absolutely hated it.

My first-grade teacher, on the other hand, just couldn't seem to get enough of it. At least a few times a week during recess she would assemble my class in a circle and then pick out a "farmer" to stand in the middle of everyone else. The farmer picked his wife; the wife picked a child; and a nurse, a dog, a cat, and a mouse followed closely behind. Together they danced around the middle of the circle as the rest of the class sang, "Hi-ho, the dairy-oh."

And then came the most sickening moment a seven-year-old could imagine: Somebody was chosen to be the cheese.

The cheese, you see, is the final person picked in The Farmer in the Dell. Upon being chosen, he or she comes from the outer ring and into the center, and then everyone else leaves. At the end of the game, then, the cheese is left all alone in the middle of a big circle of people, who stare and chant, "The cheese stands alone," over and over.

I can only remember one instance when I had to be the cheese, but once was definitely enough. The rest of my class went on with their "hi-ho, the dairy-ohs," thankful that they were not the person left in the center of the circle. I smiled the entire time, pretending that I wasn't completely crushed by what had just happened. Deep down inside, though, I was coming up with a way to get revenge on the evil mouse who had picked me.

I can picture it even now: a little frizzy-haired version of myself standing awkwardly (and angrily) in the middle of my first-grade class. My arms hung clumsily to my sides as I tried to figure out what phony facial expression would best convey the confidence that I did not feel inside.

Thirteen or so years after my schoolyard experience, I can have a good laugh at myself and at that whole situation. But back then it was just plain horrible. I hated nothing more than being left all alone.

It's funny how history repeats itself.

Round Two

My crush on Jay began the moment I first spotted him. His quick smile and noticeable height caught my attention during the first week of college, and I kept my eyes peeled for an opportunity to meet him. As it turned out, only a few days later we ended up working at the same job and sitting *right next to each other.* I could hardly believe it.

As the year wore on, a friendship grew between the two of us. My crush grew too. In casual conversations and random meetings with Jay, I tried to be as charming as possible without ever reaching the point of blatant flirtation. I did everything I could think of to help him discover that I was, of course, perfect for him. But despite all my efforts and all my intentions, our relationship didn't progress the way that I wanted it to.

And then, in the second half of the school year, the staff of our office made plans to go to a fancy event together. A week before the big night, Jay and I were chatting about it, and he proclaimed, "I'm going to need a date for this thing, aren't I?"

My heart skipped a beat. At last he had come to his senses!

Instantly I pictured myself in an elegant satin gown, floating out of a car toward Jay's outstretched hand. The words "happily ever after" came to mind, and to this day I swear I could hear a violin concerto playing in the background somewhere.

Everything seemed to be working toward a singular pivotal moment in my life when, with his eyes shining down at me, Jay said, "I think I already know who I'm going to ask."

I felt as if I were at a Hollywood awards show, waiting for the guy to open an envelope and pronounce *L-I-S-A*. My pulse was racing inside of me. Could this really be true?

Jay offered an excited little smile and promptly said, "I'm going to ask Rebecca."

Immediately the images in my head snapped into oblivion, and I felt my body revert to the same posture it had when I was a seven-year-old at the end of that schoolyard game. My stance became awkward once again, and I allowed my hands to drop clumsily to my sides. The only thing I could think of was that I didn't want my face to betray how I really felt inside.

Once again, I had been left all alone.

Crush-Colored Glasses

A similar incident occurred when I was five, involving a boy named Adam and a fuzzy pair of pink pajamas. Another one happened when I was eight; that time the boy's name was Greg. At fourteen it was Kevin.

How could I have ever thought ... ?

There wasn't really anything new or different about the situation with Jay, you see. Just like all of those other guys, he was perfectly innocent—completely oblivious to all my feeble attempts at flirting. He never once gave me a reason to think that he was interested in me. He never even knew that I was offering him a piece of my heart. To him I was a good friend, and nothing more than that.

I was looking through crush-colored glasses, though, which changed everything. I misinterpreted his friendly gestures because I wanted them to be more than what they really were. Every time he talked to me, I let myself think that it was because *he* had a crush on *me*—and I let myself believe those things because I wanted to believe them. And I wanted to believe those things because I wanted to stop being the cheese—the one who's all alone in the middle of everybody.

Watch Those Petals

Life would be so much easier if the guys we like would always like us back. It would be even better if they would always like us *first*. Tragically, though, they haven't figured out how to do either of these things. And in the meantime, young women everywhere are plucking flower petals and hoping that "He loves me" will someday come true.

If only the petals could warn us. It can be devastating to discover that "he loves me not."

Getting turned down by guys has made me question virtually everything about myself—from the size of my thighs to the sound of my voice. In my extreme moments I have resorted to a variety of compulsive behaviors: crying into my pillow, tearing photographs, ripping journal entries to shreds (my personal favorite), and crossing out entire heart-filled pages of my yearbooks.

When my destructive feelings subside, and I put the magic markers back where they belong, the only things that remain are a few collapsed journal covers and piles of ruined snapshots. And confusion. And disappointment. And hurting. In the midst of such a mess, I sit on the floor with a box of tissues and try to fight against my long-standing doubts and fears: *How could I have ever thought that he would want someone like me?*

Unsolicited Answers

Sometimes, as I watch a couple walk away in their little bubble of affection, I catch myself in an almost-prayer: *Lord, when will I forget what loneliness feels like?*

The main reason why I call this an *almost-prayer* is because it's not a real prayer. Basically, it's just me sulking and trying to pass it off as spirituality. I'm not really talking to God; I'm talking to myself. And I know that I'm not talking to God because I don't really want to hear His opinion on the matter.

What's funny about an almost-prayer is that God usually gives His opinion even though I don't want it. In the case of this particular almost-prayer, God's answer comes in the form of Bible verses that I've known since the second grade.

"God is love," Lisa, He says. (In case you're wondering, that's from 1 John 4:8.)

I let out a slow sigh and wait for a moment. *But, Lord,* I respond, *You don't send a dozen roses for my birthday.*

"This is how we know what love is," He says. *"Jesus Christ laid down his life."* (That one's from 1 John 3:16.)

A pause.

But, Lord, I reply, *You don't squeeze my hand in a dark movie theater.*

"How great is the love the Father has lavished," He says (1 John 3:1).

Another pause.

I know, Lord, but You don't write me sappy notes when I'm feeling down.

"Love comes from God," He says. (That's 1 John 4:7.)

Yes, Lord, but You don't carve my initials into an oak tree.

"For God so loved the world," He says, *"that he gave his one and only Son"* (John 3:16).

I know You love me, Lord, I say. *But why don't I feel it?*

Plugs and Seals

Many of us women make romantic connections based on the hope that a guy's smile or caring touch will fill up the lonely echo that we have inside us. When we feel bleak and barren, all we know is that attention from a guy will make us feel better about ourselves.

Loneliness can rip right through a person. It just *consumes,* doesn't it?

I have seen loneliness wreak havoc in the lives of many young women whom I hold dear. I have watched some of my closest friends get into unhealthy relationships with guys, just to alleviate their feelings of solitude. They get into relationship after relationship after short-term relationship, always with the wish that they'll stop feeling so empty inside.

There's nothing like a guy's coat draped around a girl's shoulders to relieve the cold loneliness she feels inside. The problem is that the loneliness only lifts for a moment. When the dates and the dinners are all over, she goes right back to where she started. In fact, she often winds up deeper into loneliness than she was before.

If we have nothing permanent in place to fill our hearts with joy, we naturally will seek temporary and less satisfying things to distract us from the holes we have inside. Many women use relationships with men to try to plug up these holes, but the results are far from favorable. We cannot expect a man to come in and make us whole; only something perfect and permanent can do that.

Only our Maker can seal our hearts completely. Only He can close up all of the crevices in our hearts.

C.S. Lewis said it like this:

God made us: invented us as a man invents an engine. A car is made to run on gasoline, and it would not run properly on anything else. Now, God designed the human machine to run on Himself. He Himself is the fuel our spirits were designed to burn, or the food our spirits were designed to feed on. There is no other.... God cannot give us a happiness and peace apart from Himself, because it is not there. There is no such thing.[1]

Singer Jaci Velasquez had this to say about loneliness: "God has left an open space in my life so he can enter it and fill it up.... When I feel the loneliest, I need to reach out and hang on tightly to Him. I know He'll be there. And I know He'll never, ever leave me alone."[2]

God can take our loneliness away and fill it with a companionship that is unmatched in the universe. Even though God shows His love with things that can't be stowed in a jewelry box, the love that He offers is far above the love that we can get from another human being. As Psalm 57 says, God's love reaches all the way to the heavens![3]

If we expect a mere man's affection to do God's job, we are setting the poor guy up for a serious failure, and we are setting ourselves up for a serious disappointment.

Diamonds: A Girl's Best Friend

Think about this for a second: If someone were to offer you the choice between a diamond and an everyday stone, which would you choose? It would be the diamond, wouldn't it? After all, why would someone choose a common rock over something of immense worth?

When we're dealing with things that have price tags, it's very easy to make the correct value judgments. When we're dealing with things that cannot be seen or touched, though, our decisions get much more difficult. So then, we often let spiritual things—things of great value—slip through our fingers.

Each day God offers us a diamond's wealth of the best kind of love. He gives us things out of complete unselfishness, total grace, and forgiveness that never stops. What's more, He throws in His perfect character.

Sadly, when we are faced with God's offer, we often choose only the everyday stone's quota of love. Over and over we settle for the second-rate version.

I want to rely on the best kind of love, don't you? I don't want to be the kind of person who has a nervous breakdown every time a guy reacts to me differently than I want him to. I don't want to feel as if my world is falling apart whenever Mr. Wonderful decides that I'm not his perfect match. And I don't want to rely on my journal-ripping skills to make me feel better.

We should not expect to receive our feelings of worth from any one person. Our worth comes from our Maker. As author Max Lucado writes, "Only when we find him will we be satisfied."[4]

In Christ we can be confident that we have found the best kind of love, no matter what the guys around us have to offer. And then, whether we've got a romance or a rejection letter, we're doing OK. Because, as E.H. Chapin wrote, "under the shadow of earthly disappointment, all unconscious to ourselves, our Divine Redeemer is walking by our side."

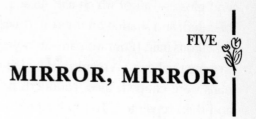

FIVE

MIRROR, MIRROR

Charm is deceptive, and beauty is fleeting; but a woman who fears the Lord is to be praised.

PROVERBS 31:30

Waving my fingers in the air to help set their shiny polish, I mentally checked off the list that had been compounding in my head all morning.

Hair? *Check.*

Clothes? *Check.*

Fingernails? *Check.*

Jewelry? *Check.*

Makeup? *Check, check.*

I glanced up at the clock on the wall, baffled. *Surely there can't be much else left to do,* I thought, but I was mistaken. The work continued at a frenzied pace. Not that it bothered me. I had never before felt so pampered.

My morning "get ready" routine had been delegated to a team of experts for the day. Highly trained professionals (each armed with scented French products) were taking care of every beauty detail that they could possibly think of. One woman had brought an arsenal of creams, shadows, pencils, and glosses—all of which she subsequently applied, blotted, blended, and shaded on my skin. A beautician styled my ever-rebellious hair. (Poor woman—it took six different techniques to tame the beast.) A manicurist had made sure that my fingernails were clipped, filed, rounded, painted, dried, stripped, and then repainted. To top it all off, someone had even tied the laces of my shoes for me.

Every imaginable detail had been covered, and there was hardly a task left for me to call my own. So, with a smile and a contented sigh, I settled into my only real job of the morning: turning my face toward the light and smacking my lips together on the command to "blot."

A New Me?

It was a once-in-a-lifetime day, and my makeover was just the beginning of it all. I was about to get my picture taken for the cover of a national magazine! Words can't even describe the thrill I felt inside. Sitting on my princess-for-a-day seat, surrounded by an excited buzz of activity, I tried to take it all in without pinching myself in disbelief.

When the makeover session neared an end, I became anxious to view the fruit of all that primping labor. (To be honest, I was concerned that I would look like a fluffed poodle.) Given a few seconds to see what I looked like, I cautiously stepped in front of a full-length mirror.

To say that I did a double take would be a severe understatement. The image that shone back at me was unlike any reflection that my body had ever produced. From the tips of my toes to the height of my hair, everything seemed to have a new sparkle and shine. My eyes seemed bluer than ever, my complexion shimmered, and my smile radiated with freshness. I hardly recognized myself.

It was like a butterfly's emergence from her cocoon. I instantly felt feminine and attractive and pretty—no, *beautiful*. In fact, if truth be told, I had never felt as stunning as I did at that moment. The beauty people practically had to drag me away from the mirror, because I just couldn't get enough of myself.

The Not-So-Real Deal

A few months later I was checking our mailbox four times a day, as the magazine was scheduled to arrive anytime. I was tickled at the chance to be able to see the final product, and the vanity in me was itching to show people just how good I could look.

When the issue finally showed up, I practically pounced on it. There was my name on the front cover, right next to a picture that had been taken at the pinnacle of my smile.

Standing next to our mailbox, I squinted my eyes to get a closer look at the face that smiled out from beneath the magazine's logo. The complexion looked smooth and even; the teeth were gleaming white contrasted against pale peach lipstick; the eyes beamed brightly from the page; and the hair curled in a way that I had never been able to achieve with my own styling products. Things looked great.

In fact, they looked a little bit too great.

With a slight glance over each shoulder, I tucked the magazine under my arm and headed toward my house. Once inside, I quickly walked into the bathroom and locked the door behind me. Then, as I stared into the mirror, I pulled my magazine out and held it up, right next to my face.

For a moment or two I simply looked. My eyes darted from the photograph of my face to my face, then back, making little comparisons between the two images. As I took everything in, I couldn't help but notice that the photograph looked much better than the real thing.

I smiled as much as I possibly could, trying to re-create the look on the magazine cover. I opened my eyes wide and even tried a little laugh. But after only a few attempts, my face fell, and a lump began to develop in the back of my throat. I turned away from the mirror and stared at the magazine once more. *Face it, Lisa,* I thought, *you don't look half that good in real life.*

My stomach began to churn. Then, almost as quickly, I became angry at myself because I didn't feel happy. *You should be excited,* I scolded. *Good grief, your face is plastered on a magazine cover! There are girls who would do anything to have that opportunity.*

Call me crazy, but I couldn't redirect the course that my brain was on. I had begun to worry about what other people might think when they saw the magazine cover. Would my friends notice the differences that I had noticed? Would my family? Would other people make the same comparisons that I had made? Worst of all, would they come to the same conclusion that I had come to?

The idea alone made me ill to the core.

The Aftermath

The next day I woke up an hour earlier than usual so I would have time to get ready for school. I put on my favorite outfit, spent forty-five minutes applying makeup, and even borrowed my sister's curling iron for my hair. When I was finally ready to go, I glanced into the mirror one last time.

Well, this will just have to do, I thought, turning toward the door.

At school that day everything seemed normal until my third-period class rolled around. I was sitting at my desk, waiting for the teacher to show up, when one of the girls in the class pulled a magazine out of her backpack—*the* magazine.

Instantly I slouched in my seat and pretended not to notice what was going on. The girl with the magazine beamed a smile my way and held up the picture of my face. Then, with her voice filling the entire classroom, she made an excited little announcement.

"Hey, guys," she proclaimed, "look what I've got!"

As my classmates turned to see, I slouched deeper into my chair. Then my worst fear became reality: The magazine started circulating.

For the next five minutes the glossy picture of me made its way around the room. As my peers looked at the photograph, I was pretending not to notice. But in reality I was scrutinizing every single one of their reactions. From facial expressions to breathing patterns, I noticed the slightest change. And each change made me worry.

I felt ridiculously paranoid, but I couldn't stop myself. *They must see it too,* I kept thinking. *They must think that I'm absolutely hideous in real life.*

For the remainder of the class period I tried not to make eye contact with anyone. When the bell rang to signal the end of the hour, I bolted from my seat and rushed out the door.

It was all in my brain. I knew it. My classmates hadn't said or done anything mean or hurtful or even noticeable. Still, as I squeezed my body through crowded hallways toward the ladies' room, a familiar nagging voice resonated in my head. Without warning it had returned once again, and now it would not let up: *You're not pretty, you're not pretty, you're not pretty.*

The Beholder's Eye

The Bible says that "we are God's masterpiece,"[1] but sometimes I just don't feel that way. In fact, one of the most exhausting tasks that I face in life is learning how to be satisfied with my appearance.

As I look in the mirror each morning, I usually feel more like a melted crayon than a stunning work of art. My eyes are too narrow, my lips too thin, my hair too poofy, my eyebrows the wrong color. My calf muscles won't firm up, and my thighs won't shrink. My waist is too big, my hips are too big, and my feet are too big.

No matter how nicely my hair curls or how smooth my skin feels, I can always find something that I'd like to improve about my appearance. I want to have a haircut that frames my face better, a complexion that harvests fewer zits, eyebrows that arch a little more, and fingernails that grow together in unison. I want my teeth to be whiter, my ears to be more symmetrical, and my knees to be more rounded.

It feels as if I'm on a treadmill run that won't ever come to an end. Just when I think that I can get off the track, take a breath, and say that I have actually accepted my physical appearance, I realize that my struggle is nowhere near over. Looking down, I find that my feet are still pounding out the same laborious rhythm that they have always been.

I want so much for others to think I'm beautiful.

I want so much to feel beautiful, to be beautiful.

Glitz and Glamour

A guy once told me that I have a bubble butt. At first I was offended that a male had brought up my rear end in conversation. I mean, who *does* that?

Next I became annoyed that he had actually been dense enough to *say* what he had said about it. More than anything, though, I was unnerved at the tone of disapproval that had accompanied his use of the word *bubble*.

Upon returning home that day, I spent half an hour checking out my rear in a mirror, thinking, *Maybe I should try to hide it. Would skirts help? Perhaps I should wear more black.*

Somehow, over the course of my life on this planet, I have convinced myself that everything will fall into place when I eventually learn to look my best. When I finally get that perfect haircut, Mr. Wonderful will take notice of me. With just the right outfit, all of those girls will realize that I'm good enough for their group. And maybe if I lose a few pounds, I'll begin to feel better about myself.

Now, compared to most young women, I wouldn't be

considered "sensitive" about my appearance. But like any normal woman, there have been times when I could be described
as slightly thin-skinned—my magazine experience being one
of the more obvious instances. I have been insulted by com-
pliments and hurt by flattery. On occasion I have taken offense
at something that's not even remotely unkind. (Once, when a
person *didn't* tell me that I looked nice, I burst into tears.)

Indeed, I have had my moments, but for the most part I feel
semi-OK about the way I look. You see, I know deep down that
all of my glitz and glamour lasts about as long as a Popsicle in
the Gobi Desert. At the end of the day, when I lie on my bed
with two slimy cucumber slices over my eyes, I am reminded
that none of my primping efforts have ever improved anything.

Which is pretty pathetic, because it's ridiculous to think of
all the things I do for the sake of looking good. I buy creams
to zap my zits and makeup to cover the creams. I've purchased
mascara in bulk because I want my eyelashes to look thicker,
and I keep thinking that blush will give me cheekbones. For
the times when those things fail, I have gloss to fall back on,
because it makes everything sparkle like Christmas.

As if all of that weren't enough, I have dressing room tricks
that would make Hollywood jealous. My bureaus are filled
with corsets to shrink my waistline and pantyhose to keep my
cellulite hidden. I have control tops, push-ups, shapers, mini-
mizers, maximizers, and gravity-defiers. I put myself through a
rigorous routine of daily exercises. Like a peppy little aerobics
instructor, I cheer and cheer:

Shoulders back, head up!

Purse those lips. Now smile!

You *can* resist that third brownie!

Suck it in, suck it in, *SUCK IT IN!*

Round and round I go, doing everything I can possibly do to be beautiful. Time spent, money spent, energy spent—anything to look better. And all the while, like a glaring screensaver for my head, "Beauty is on the inside" keeps on scrolling.

A Step Back From the Mirror

The best makeover in the world and the most talented stylists on the planet cannot cover up an ugly spirit. Unhappiness and discontent can slice through any outfit, and the thickest concealer on the market cannot hide a troubled heart. Designer jeans and a diamond necklace can't distract from a soul that is not at peace. Looking good on the outside is no use at all if the inside doesn't look good, because our inner self always outshines our outer appearance.

Have you ever noticed how people you like always seem prettier than people you don't like? It's true, and nice girls always seem better looking than mean ones. You see, no matter how much we try to look put together and beautiful, it won't matter if we don't keep our internal self intact and looking good.

The Bible tells us, "The Lord does not look at the things man looks at. Man looks at the outward appearance, but the Lord looks at the heart."[2] Isn't this encouraging? It's so nice for me to know that, when God looks at me, He's not checking out my cheekbones, my hairstyle, or my waistline. He's looking at the thing that makes me who I am—my heart.

From God's point of view, "pretty" does not have anything to do with my physical appearance. In His perspective "pretty" describes qualities of character: things like kindness, love, patience, unselfishness, wisdom, and grace. The Bible says that our beauty should come from the "inner self."[3] This means that we should be focusing on our *spirit* more than our *looks*.

One woman put it this way: "The joy that shines through from having a love relationship with Christ is what makes a person truly beautiful."[4] So as much as I want people to think I'm gorgeous, I should *really* want God to think that I look good.

Now, just as God's definition of "pretty" describes a person's character, so does His definition of "ugly." From God's perspective, an ugly person is someone filled with ugly character: things like jealousy, greed, pride, and arrogance. And discontent.

Ridding our lives of discontent can be extremely difficult, but it's important to do so—even when it comes to the area of physical appearance. When we turn up our noses at our own reflection, we're also turning up our noses at the One who created that reflection.

Fight the Good Fight

Here are a few ways to fight discontent in everyday life:

1. **Don't look in the mirror until you can be happy with what shines back at you.** Thinking negative thoughts about your reflection will only breed more discontent in your heart. As Philippians 4:8 says, we should think about things that are

"right," "pure," "lovely," "admirable," "excellent," and "praiseworthy." (And seriously, thinking things like, *My butt is so huge,* is not very lovely or praiseworthy.)

2. **Resist the urge to compare yourself to a supermodel.** You'll never be happy with your appearance if you're constantly comparing yourself to someone who's airbrushed. And you won't be happy even if you're comparing yourself to the girl next door, who happens to be skinnier, taller, shorter, curvier, or somehow *better* than you.

3. **Learn to accept the things that you cannot change.** Unlike some of my friends, I will never have cute, small feet. Apart from a miracle of modern science, my skin won't ever really tan. My hair will most likely always grow from my head as a tangled red mess.

   These are things that I won't be able to change about myself, so I may as well learn to see the beauty in them. I remind myself that curly hair saves me $40 a month in perm fees. And I couldn't be tall—which spreads out the fat—without such big feet.

4. **Change the things that are unhealthy.** It's hard to feel good about yourself—especially your physical appearance— when you're not taking care of yourself the way that you should be. Should you
   • gain some weight?
   • lose a few pounds?
   • eat healthier?
   • get more sleep?

- resist certain habits?
- throw away certain products?
- exercise more?
- let go of "friends" who only tear you down?

5. **Do what you can to make the most of things.** As my mom says, "Play up the good points!" Buy clothing that highlights the things you like most about your figure. Get a haircut that accentuates your high cheekbones, your cute nose, or your long eyelashes. If you want to wear makeup, wear what emphasizes your favorite facial features. Still, remember this great quote I recently ran across: "It's doubtful that God wants us to spend half the morning covering up the faces He intentionally blessed us with."[5]

6. **Appreciate the unique things about your own body.** As one book says, "accept who you are and revel in that."[6] Stand up for yourself, even if it's just to say that you like your boyish figure or your flat feet. Some people turn up their noses to pale features, but I happen to like being fair-skinned. Now I dare to say so, and it feels great.

The Fairest One of All

One of my first experiences with my friend Sandra was "Residence Life Week" at my college campus. "Res-Life," as everyone called it, was a seven-day period of time set aside to build community among students at our school. It consisted of a whole bunch of activities that people could embarrass themselves in: a cardboard boat race across the pond, a water balloon-launching competition, and a pudding tug-of-war. Every hall from each dorm could participate in the events, earning points toward a big prize at the end of the week.

Now, I have never been one to sign up for personal humiliation, and I don't get a special thrill out of pudding in my hair or pond scum on my clothes. For these reasons I avoided Res-Life activities like the plague, pretending not to notice the brightly colored sign-up sheets just outside my door.

Sandra, on the other hand, chose to represent my dorm in almost every activity. She rode a miniature bicycle through a maze of orange construction cones, ate a frosted donut as it dangled from a string, and pulled a rope over a huge mess of chocolate pudding. And she did each of these with a big laugh and a huge smile.

Over time I got to know Sandra better, and we became good friends. In some ways, I found, she was just like most of the other girls I knew: She liked to shop, she liked guys, she worried about her clothes and her hair, and she really liked to have fun. Beyond all those things, though, I could tell that there was something really special about her.

Sandra had a servant's heart like none I had ever seen before. She was constantly looking out for other people and trying to make them feel good.

If it was someone's birthday, Sandra would make a sign and blow up balloons to surprise her. When a group of people got together, she would always bring snacks to share. When a bunch of girls gathered to watch a beauty pageant on TV, Sandra showed up with crowns—made out of sparkly silver pipe cleaners—for everyone to wear. Once, at the end of a group shopping excursion, Sandra surprised everyone with a box of gourmet chocolates, just to say "thanks" for a great day.

Such generosity and selflessness is infectious. Others get inspired to give of themselves because they see how great it is to be served.

It's people like my friend Sandra who show the rest of the world what *real* beauty is. With someone like her around, everything changes. She reminds me that outer beauty is worthless without an inner radiance to back it up. At the end of the day, when all of the shimmer and shine have been rinsed down the drain, it is beauty like Sandra's that lasts.

Beauty School Dropout

If you feel that you have "problem areas" and "figure flaws," you are not alone. Natalie thinks that her teeth are too crooked. Andrea says that she's too tall. Katie thinks she has "man feet," and Laura dislikes her acne scars. Heather isn't happy with how much she weighs, and Jaclyn says that her eyelashes are terrible.

Let's try not to get hung up on those things, OK? Let's seek to avoid being what 2 Corinthians calls "those who take pride in what is seen rather than in what is in the heart."[7] Let's remember that true beauty is not found in the size of a waist or the symmetry of a face. It can't be found in a compact, a tube, or a pair of designer jeans. It rests in the heart and shines forth from there. It is something that endures through time.

Thank goodness.

When I was a freshman in high school, I got a little

overzealous one day while plucking my eyebrows, and I ended up with a space between them that was big enough to drive a truck through. I attempted to fill in the gap with a pencil that didn't match my face or eyebrows, which only made things worse. I ended up looking as if I belonged on the set of *Halloween XIV.* I had to put myself on Tweezer Probation for the next eight weeks.

As much as I like to look nice, I truly hope that I'm better at weeding out ugliness in my soul than I am at maintaining the arches of my eyebrows.

SIX

A LITTLE BLACK DRESS

Like a gold ring in a pig's snout is a beautiful woman who shows no discretion.

PROVERBS 11:22

I t was a floor-length formal dress with spaghetti straps, a slit that went up to *there*, a bust line that was much lower than normal for me, and a back that was almost entirely cut out. I tried it on, did a little spin in front of the dressing room mirrors, and grinned widely at the reflections.

The dress fit perfectly. It made me feel glamorous, sexy, and grown-up. To my delight, I already owned shoes that would match it perfectly, and its price had been marked down more than 50 percent.

I bought the dress.

To say the least, this purchase was uncharacteristic of me. I'm usually the girl who gets told to "lighten up" on shopping excursions, because my definition of modesty is a lot stricter than that of most young women my age. In fact, many of my peers avoid asking my opinion on certain outfits because they know exactly what I'll say: "Too clingy, too low, too short, too revealing." You get the picture.

The very act of buying The Dress went against most of what I stood for and claimed to value. But I did it anyway.

Reason Gone Wrong

It had been one of those days (weeks, months) that seem to come around for me periodically. I had been feeling down about not having a boyfriend, and more than anything, I wanted to believe that I could be attractive to the opposite sex. I figured that the easiest way to reach that goal was to walk around in something slightly low-cut and formfitting (OK, scratch the *slightly*).

To be completely honest, I was hoping that my new dress would somehow—magically, of course—land me in a relationship. I teased myself with the notion that modesty was the thing that was keeping guys away from me, and I hoped with all my heart that a plunging neckline would be my ticket to at least a few dates.

With that dream in mind, I waited expectantly for an opportunity to show off my new, eye-catching self. It was only a few weeks later that I had the chance to wear The Dress. A group of my girlfriends and I made plans to go to a show one evening, all dolled up in formal attire. This, I decided, would be my night to shine.

When the time came, I pinned my hair to the top of my head and put on my strappy high-heeled shoes. I made sure that my makeup was shimmering and flawless, and I tossed a tube of lipstick into my purse for good measure. Then, to top everything off, I slipped into the most revealing thing that I had ever worn in public.

Hours later, the evening over, I replaced my little black number with a T-shirt and a pair of pajama pants. I walked over to my closet with the dress in hand and paused for a moment, debating what I should do with it. Then, with a frustrated sigh, I scrunched the thing into a ball and threw it into the deepest corner of my closet, back behind a dusty pair of boots. For all I cared, it could sit there in a heap forever. It certainly wasn't worth wasting a hanger on.

A Not-So-Happy Ending

Things did not happen the way that I had thought they would that night. I had anticipated showing the world a whole new side of myself, and I had hoped that wearing my "fabulous" new gown would result in a memorable evening for me. What I hadn't expected, though, was the kind of memories that I actually ended up with.

Throughout the entire evening I was nervous and uncomfortable because of what I was wearing. When I bent over even slightly, I had to grab the front of my dress to keep from having my entire chest exposed. I was perpetually worried about whether my dress had shifted, because that could have been, well, dangerous. I had to sit down *very* carefully so that my underwear wouldn't show at the base of my back, and I was constantly fighting that slit at my thigh.

There were other things to worry about too. Every time a guy even glanced in my general direction, I wanted to crawl into a hole. *What is he looking at?*

I spent the majority of the night with my back to a wall and both arms crossed over my chest. I didn't have a single coed conversation. In fact, I think that if a guy *had* approached me, I probably would have branded him a complete sleazebag.

All of my hopes for extra attention had quickly fallen by the wayside, and I was feeling very miserable and very upset. Where had I gone wrong? What could I have done differently? I had only wanted to feel attractive, but somehow the situation had gotten way out of control.

Back to the Dressing Room

As you've probably guessed, I occasionally have a difficult time with modesty in my way of dress. Sure, I'm more modest than a lot of my friends, but at times I can't even seem to figure out what modesty is. There are moments when I wonder if it is really important or if it's just one of those rules that adults have used to brainwash their children. And there are days when I want to completely rebel against traditional dress codes, proclaiming that "Christianity is freedom!" in a miniskirt, a tube top, and go-go boots.

But something holds me back.

Despite all of the mutinous ideas that crisscross my brain, there is a heaviness in my gut with regard to this issue, and the feeling just doesn't seem to go away. I have an inkling, you see, that under all of those ridiculous "three inches above the knee and no spaghetti straps" rules, a *real* principle can be found— a valuable principle. And so I have this nagging suspicion that what I put on my body really *does* matter—that modesty really *is* important somehow.

The Abandoned Virtue

It's easy for me to neglect the issue of modesty in the way I dress. My brain just doesn't go there automatically. In choosing an outfit for the day, I'm most likely to be concerned about whether or not my colors coordinate. Most mornings I simply get up, rifle through a bunch of "nothing to wear," and eventually pick something that will (hopefully) make me look good.

Aha—that's where the problem comes in. Some of the stuff that makes me *look good*—that is, skinnier, more attractive—might not actually *be good* to wear in public.

A perfect example of this is my very own little black dress. When I initially put the thing on, I thought I looked great. It made me look thin in places that I wanted to be thin and curvy in places that I wanted to be curvy. I fully approved of the fact that it covered my stomach, hid my thighs, and showed off my collarbones. But what I failed to pay enough attention to was the way in which it did such things.

My little black dress, you see, had been strategically manufactured to show off the sexual features of the female body. Between its dip at my chest, its scoop at my back, its clingy fabric, and its notice-me slit, the dress practically screamed, "Hey, guys, look at *this!*"

Believe me, the people who designed the thing knew exactly what they were doing.

Lions and Tigers and Boys, Oh, My!

Now, the subject of lust and the male sex drive always makes me feel a bit like a piece of raw meat. I get uncomfortable because I don't know what to do with the feelings it causes. It makes me feel gross and dirty and guilty and suspicious and used inside. But it needs to be brought up.

It has been said that the most sexual organ on a man's body is his eye. What he sees has a very big effect on what he thinks, and visual images of the female body can cause a guy's brain to jump straight into lust mode. When we women wear clothing that displays too much flesh or a close silhouette of our figures, we are taking advantage of a weakness that many men find difficult to control.

Don't just take my word for it, though. Here's what a few guys had to say about the way girls dress:

> The style of clothes a woman wears has a major impact on how men look at her. If a woman wants men to treat her with respect, she should show respect for them by dressing appropriately, among other things.
>
> —Chris

> Women shouldn't be ashamed to look pretty and dress to impress, but excess cleavage and skin-showy outfits are not safe.
>
> —Stevan

> Immodest dress causes the arousal of sexual thoughts and ideas in men that should not be filling our heads. We

do not need women to feed our sexual desires.

—Matt

A girl can't simply dress according to what she feels is right, because what she feels is right for her might not be right for a guy to look at.

—Nate[1]

How a woman dresses is a direct reflection of her values. A modest woman shows that she respects the thought life of those around her.

—Kory

When you dress modestly, we're not thinking, "Where'd she find that, Goodwill?" Believe me, we're thinking, "Whew! Finally, a girl who's smart enough not to flaunt it." Seriously. I promise that's what we're thinking!

—Rory[2]

Whose Responsibility?

OK, OK, guys want us to dress modestly. But really, is that even fair of them to ask? After all, shouldn't *they* be the ones who are responsible for the way they think?

Well, yes and no. It *is* a guy's responsibility to keep his mind pure—period. Even so, we women have the opportunity to assist and encourage men in that purity.

As my friend Chelsea pointed out, we can think of the guys around us as our brothers—some are even our brothers in

Christ. As these men grow up and (hopefully) mature, they will end up marrying our female friends and sisters in Christ. At the very least, we should strive for modesty out of respect for those women, our future friends-in-law. Just like you and me, they are people who long to find a love that is pure and untarnished.

Think about this one for a second: Wouldn't it be great if there were modest women around your future mate right now—women who seek to help *your future husband* keep his thoughts pure? Imagine the possibilities! Right now, the way that *they* dress could be affecting the way that *your* groom thinks.

As Romans 12:10 (NLT) says, we should "take delight in honoring each other." For this reason, we should show some consideration for the men around us—consideration for the types of thoughts that can go through their heads. By dressing modestly, we show them that we value the difficult task of keeping a pure thought life. It is a way to demonstrate respect and support for the guys in our lives.

The story doesn't end there, though, because modesty doesn't just benefit the guys around us. It benefits us too.

Girl Power

Choosing to be modest is a very empowering thing. It is a sign that a person is confident and secure. While some women rely on low necklines to catch the attention of others, a modest woman depends on inner, lasting qualities to set herself apart from the rest. While immodest women showcase the cheapest versions of themselves first, a modest woman forces the world to see her internal value too.

Some women argue that baring a lot of flesh is simply a sign that they are "proud of their bodies" and "comfortable in their own skin." Well, we should all strive for a certain level of comfort with the way we look. However, along with the public display of pride and comfort that these women claim to be exhibiting, they are also subtly suggesting that their exterior deserves more attention than their interior.

When we don't feel beautiful on the inside, it's likely that we'll rely too heavily on our physical charms in relationships. When we're convinced that we have little or no internal allure, it's easy to believe that a primal physical union is the only thing that we could ever get out of a relationship. We resort to immodesty, then, because we believe that it is our final hope for gaining male approval.

We won't get much more than that, though, because relationships of substance are never based on purely physical things. If we allow body parts other than our mouths to do most of the talking for us, the majority of our conversations will not occur with men of character. So, in the search for the man of your dreams, modesty will help to keep the best guys at the center of your selection process.

As Ephesians 5:15 (NLT) says, we should "be careful how [we] live, not as fools but as those who are wise." This fits directly into a discussion of modesty. Even though dressing suggestively may gain us a few approving glances from the opposite sex, a *wise* woman knows that the kind of guy who constantly chases after short skirts is not exactly Prince Charming.

As my newly married friend Jaclyn pointed out, "Girls who flaunt what they've got are sure to attract guys, but not ones who care about their personalities." Another young woman put it this way: "A girl will attract a certain kind of young man by the way she dresses. If a woman's desire is to have a godly mate, it only makes sense that that kind of man would value modesty, not only in dress but also in speech and presence."

I don't know about you, but I'm searching for a mate who looks at women with respect—a man who values my heart more than my measurements. Even though the vanity in me wants my husband to think that I'm hot, I want him to love me based on who I am rather than how I look in a skirt. In order to find such a person, my inner qualities should be the things that I put on center stage.

But enough of all that deep stuff for a while.

On a Shallow Note

Modesty is great for many virtuous reasons, but one of my favorite things about modesty is that it is *always* in style. You won't ever have to surrender your fashion sense to have a closet that's stocked full of modest clothes. Even though showing skin seems to be permanently *in*, it will always be OK to take a more covered-up approach.

We don't have to be swathed in burlap sacks from head to toe in order to be dressed appropriately. We don't have to wear Victorian styles either—flowing skirts, long sleeves, and lace up to our chins. Our bathing suits do not need to be knee-length, and hoop skirts are completely out of the question. As one writer noted, "modesty is very different from prudery."[3]

Modest clothes can be found on the hottest fashion runways all around the world. At every Hollywood awards show (a.k.a. *style fest*), there are outfits that don't cling and outfits that don't reveal too much. From the boutiques of Rodeo Drive in Los Angeles to the shops of Fifth Avenue in New York City, modesty always has a strong showing. (If you don't believe me, pick up a fashion magazine and see for yourself!)

If modesty is the goal, then, the project becomes very simple, because there are plenty of options available.

To Buy or Not to Buy

There are really only two things to remember when you're trying to dress modestly: *fit* and *coverage*.

1. **Make sure that your clothing fits you correctly.** Here are a few things to think about:
   - *A bad gap.* When purchasing button-down shirts, make sure that they're the right size. The buttons should lie flat down the middle. Thus you avoid unintentionally flashing people, and you won't have to worry about having chilly gusts of wind blow across your chest.
   - *Lamaze for beginners?* When zipping up a pair of pants requires special breathing exercises, it's a sign that the pants are too tight. Usually one size bigger will be a good fit (not to mention the fact that you'll actually be able to walk).

- *The wrinkle rule.* When shopping for shirts, make sure that they don't pull, crease, or wrinkle across the chest. You'll avoid drawing extra attention to that area.

2. **Make sure that your clothing covers you well.** Here are a few guidelines that may help:
   - *I see London.* If a skirt or a pair of shorts is so short that it gives others a glimpse of your underwear, it's a good idea to buy something a bit longer. (I like my underwear, but that doesn't mean everyone else should *see* it.)
   - *I see France.* If bending over gives people a full (or partial) view of a bra or worse, this is definitely a neckline to worry about. You could avoid bending over, but you'll be a lot more comfortable if you just leave this one on its hanger.
   - *I'm coming out!* Your belly button may be absolutely adorable, but that doesn't mean that it's the best accessory to every outfit in your wardrobe. Showing off too much of your abdomen often allows people to see other things that are much better off covered up.

A Modest Proposal

There are some really simple ways to incorporate fashion into life without having to shorten skirts or shrink-wrap pants. For example, trendiness can easily be achieved with the right accessories. From plastic rings to cameo necklaces, a little bit of the latest jewelry will add the perfect amount of *in* to any ensemble. Things like scarves, belts, and hats are really fun to experiment with, and the right handbag can add style too.

Even so, my personal style weakness will always be in footwear. As one woman noted, "Shoes are the exclamation point at the end of the fashion statement."[4] A sassy set of heels or a clunky twist on loafers can spice up any outfit, and there's nothing like a pair of knee-high black boots.

Fashion is always fun, even when you choose to wear clothes that aren't sexually suggestive. In fact, some of the most stylish and beautiful women I know are also some of the most modest women I have ever met. They understand that feeling attractive and looking good do not require them to wear less clothing on their bodies. Even though they may have hourglass figures and legs that don't quit, they make sure that people notice their strongest qualities first.

The Whole Truth

Now, being modest in the way that you dress will not automatically turn you into a person of character. But a habitual practice of it can make you a better person.

Here's how: modesty allows us to focus on true beauty. It is a loving gesture toward our brothers in Christ and other men in our lives. It frees us from distractions so that we can live more totally for God.

If you have character to begin with, modesty will let it come to the foreground. Wise choices in the way that you dress, speak, and act will be the perfect background for what should always take center stage: the love of Christ shining from within. And *that*, by the way, is much more attractive than anything a little black dress will ever be able to show off.

SEVEN

THAT GIRL

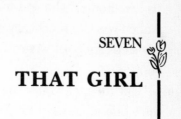

A heart at peace gives life to the body, but envy rots the bones.

PROVERBS 14:30

Underneath my eyes were two shining black smudges—the traces of mascara that had been applied eleven hours earlier—and my lipstick had faded almost completely. Two hours of cheerleading workouts had forced the gel completely out of my hair, and the remnants of a frizzy ponytail stuck out from my head in all directions.

As I slowly lumbered up our driveway, a backpack in one hand balanced the weight of the duffel bag that was slung over my opposite shoulder. I had temporarily swapped gym shoes for a pair of clogs, which looked pretty strange combined with my athletic socks. My bright yellow T-shirt was disgustingly sweaty and didn't even begin to match the blue sport shorts I was wearing.

It had been a very long day. Little did I know that it was about to get much longer.

As soon as I stepped over the threshold of our back door, my younger sister, Sarah, burst out of her upstairs bedroom.

"Is Lisa home?" she spurted almost breathlessly. The blonde sixteen-year-old practically jumped down the stairs, stopping a few steps short of where I was peeling a gym bag from my body.

"Did they tell you?" she gasped, her face bright and her voice bubbling over with glee.

I tried to get my tired eyes to reflect a little of the thrill that Sarah showed, thinking that if I humored her for a while she would soon go away and leave me to my peace and quiet. "Tell me what?" I responded.

My little sister took in an elated breath of air and let out what was somewhere between a squeal and a shriek. Her entire face shone with delight, and she vigorously declared, "I'm going on a date tonight!"

My gym bag hit the floor. I instantly forgot about the respite that I had been waiting for, and the scene in front of me began to make sense.

Yes, Sarah was definitely going out. Three steps above me was a masterpiece of hair, makeup, and clothing coordination. Everything went together flawlessly—from the sparkle on her eyelids to the silver belt buckle at her waist and the shiny trim of her shoes. She looked absolutely gorgeous.

As I stood beneath my sister, I was immediately reminded of my frizzy hair and mascara circles. This was not the best time for me to be hearing her news. It was clear that she felt completely lit up inside, while it seemed as though my life had become a continuous, lonely black hole of dateless Friday nights. Like so many times before, I really wanted what she had.

Down the Hall and a World Apart

Even when I have myself put together well, I bet you'd never guess that Sarah and I are related. About the only visible thing that my little sister and I have in common is that we are both relatively tall. There really isn't much else.

Sarah has pin-straight blonde hair; mine is red and naturally curly. I have almond-shaped light blue eyes; hers are round and dark green. In the summer Sarah can easily get a nice tan, but my skin seems to stay pure white no matter how much sunlight it gets.

Our differences extend far beyond appearances. My personality is much more outgoing than Sarah's, but she likes to go out a whole lot more than I do. I usually dress myself in classic fashion, while my little sis prefers clothes that are a bit more trendy.

Sarah is incredibly athletic, while I struggle to hold a golf club correctly. I play sports to win, though, while my sister usually just wants to have fun. Even so, she beats me in every sport from tennis to basketball—the only exception being, as she always points out, that I "throw a mean baton."

Maybe it's because the differences between us really are so great, or maybe it's simply because she grew up in the room next door to me, but my little sister has always been the person that I compare myself to most often. I look at her qualities and weigh them against mine, and in moments of weakness, it's really easy for me to get envious of her.

Purple vs. Puke

I've never really considered myself to be ugly, but sometimes I wish that I looked more like Sarah. I would love to be able to have a nose without a hump on it, great big eyes, and a rounded hairline (as opposed to my square one). If only *my* legs were as skinny at my thighs as they are at my knees.

It would be great, I tell myself, to be able to wear colors like pink and purple instead of the hues that generally look good on redheads. (I've always thought that I look best in the various shades of puke.) If only I looked like my sister.

Then there's her humor. Sarah is one of the funniest people I have ever met. I, on the other hand, have a very dry and individual sense of humor. Most of the times I make a joke, people don't even catch it. I would *love* to be able to make people laugh, to lighten up a room the way that my sister can. But I can only dream of coming up with one-liners and quips like the ones that Sarah seems to rattle off effortlessly.

And then there are all those males. Sometimes I wonder just how she does it! My little sister had to turn down three prom dates in one year and was asked out numerous other times by numerous other guys. I had reached eighteen years old and was still waiting for my first date to happen; Sarah was only sixteen on the night that she went on hers.

I don't think that I have ever been more aware of the differences between Sarah and me than I was that evening. When her date arrived to pick her up, I couldn't help but wish that a guy had stopped by to take *me* out.

As Sarah excitedly came down the stairs to meet him, *I*

longed to be the one in a smiling, nervous flurry. When he opened the door for her as they left, *I* wanted to have someone to say "thanks" to. As I watched them drive down the street, I couldn't stop thinking about the ways her life seemed better than mine. In the midst of my self-pity, there was a very dark and all-too-familiar tug on my heart.

Beauty and Me

Perhaps you're familiar with the feeling: Your chest sinks, and a lump of air gets caught in the back of your throat. Your fingers clam up, your fists clench, and your eyes become mere slits in the front of your head. Ladies, this is jealousy at work.

OK, maybe it's not always *that* awful, but it can get pretty bad, can't it?

A few years ago I came to a point in my life when I felt jealous little twinges in my chest quite frequently. During that time I was so jealous of my little sister that I couldn't bear to be anywhere near her, and the very sight of her blonde hair made me cringe. Whenever she was around, I felt horrible about myself. Her presence reminded me of all the wonderful things she was and all the wonderful things I wanted to be.

Due to my constant evaluating and perpetual comparing, I could no longer see myself as I was on my own. I only saw the ways that I didn't measure up to my sister: not as funny, not as pretty, not as popular, *et cetera*. Every time I saw Sarah, I allowed myself to feel inferior and inadequate. So I began to dislike her—a lot.

Jealousy has a peculiar and fickle way of distorting our

vision like that. We look at people whom we consider to be "ideal" and find that we just don't come close to the kind of individuals they are. We think of ourselves as lesser humans, mere substandards of a better version. We feel worse and worse about ourselves, until we are so filled with jealousy that we start to resent people for their good qualities.

Jealousy rarely starts at that point, though. It may even begin as borderline admiration. A perfectly good and complimentary realization (for example, "Her eyes are beautiful!") can lead to slight envy ("I wish I had those eyes!"), which brings out dissatisfaction in us (*"My* eyes are hideous.") and ultimately leads to total resentment ("The jerk. What did *she* do to deserve eyes like that?"). Thus we are transformed from happy little beings to complete monsters—in almost no time at all.

Sound familiar?

Getting Personal

Have you ever disliked another young woman because you secretly wanted something that she had? Have you ever narrowed your eyes with repulsion or rolled them with disgust when she walked into a room? Have you convinced yourself that *she* is the reason for all your misery and despair?

OK, now, be honest with me. Is there a Sarah Velthouse in your own life? Think about it for a second. How about

- that girl with the oh-so-perfect figure?
- that girl who got the boyfriend you wanted?
- that girl who can play five different sports?

- that girl who sings like an angel?
- that girl who has a brand-new sports car?
- that girl who always knows what to do?
- that girl who gets straight As without even trying?
- that girl who doesn't have to worry about money?
- that girl whose parents are still together?
- that girl who never has a hair out of place?
- that girl who exudes confidence everywhere she goes?
- that girl who knows how to do her makeup just right?
- that girl who always seems so happy?
- that girl who wears all the right clothes?
- that girl who gets praise from people all the time?
- that girl who has a date every weekend?
- that girl who gets along with her family?
- that girl with the perfect complexion?
- that girl who has hundreds of friends?

Oh, there are just so many qualities to be jealous about and so many girls to be jealous of!

As you read through the list (and be honest, now—nobody's watching), did any of those people ring a bell? Do you have a mental picture of someone specific in your head right this moment? Is there a "That Girl" in your life?

Do you base your worth on how you measure up to someone else? Do your eyes turn green with envy whenever *she* walks into the room? Have you been, like I was, struggling with the sin of too much comparison?

Boats and Bugs

That's right: Jealousy is *sin*. In the New Testament the apostle Paul ranks jealousy and envy right up there along with things like sexual immorality, idolatry, hatred, and drunkenness. (Check out Galatians 5:19-21.) And as Proverbs 27:4 says, "Anger is cruel and fury overwhelming, but who can stand before jealousy?"

The Bible's position on this subject is clear: Jealousy is no small matter. Still, you may ask, is it really *that bad*? Certainly other things have the potential to be much more destructive, don't they?

As a pastor once said, "If you're Noah and your ark is sinking, get rid of the elephants first—but pay attention to the termites!"[1] Just as something as obvious as too much weight will sink a ship, so will a steady deterioration of the boat's framework over time. The end result is the same: a vessel that won't go anywhere.

We should be on the lookout for *all* the things that have the power to destroy us from within. Even a "small" sin like jealousy can prevent a person from getting where he or she wants to be, so it is important for us to eliminate jealous attitudes and actions from our daily lives.

Another problem with jealousy is that it can go undetected by our built-in "sin radar." If we're not watching ourselves closely enough, jealousy will sneak up out of the darkness and grab hold of us.

But how can a person avoid jealous feelings toward someone else? And how would a person go about getting rid of such feelings?

Fruit in Motion

One of the most effective ways to combat sins like jealousy is to be equipped with weapons that naturally oppose it. A great place to start building up your arsenal can be found in Galatians 5, where Paul lists the fruit of the Spirit: faithfulness, peace, goodness, self-control, love, gentleness, patience, kindness, and joy. All of these things can be used to help heal or prevent an envious heart. Here are just a few ways to practice the virtues in everyday life:

- Be *self-controlled* enough to avoid jealousy. No one can force you to get rid of it. You must *choose* to keep it away.
- Pray for *peace* about who you are and what you have. In his book, *When God Whispers Your Name,* author Max Lucado writes, "There is a correlation between the way you feel about yourself and the way you feel about others. If you are at peace with yourself—if you like yourself— you will get along with others."
- Discover *joy* in your life—enough that you'll be satisfied without wanting what someone else has.
- *Love* people—especially those you are tempted to dislike or be jealous of. Ask God to help you see them the way He sees them.
- Practice *faithfulness* in the ways you apply the fruits of the Spirit to your thoughts and behaviors. Make them habitual!
- Show *kindness, goodness,* and *gentleness* to others. (These should flow naturally if you have the "love" part figured out!)
- Have *patience* with the process. Conquering specific sins does not usually happen overnight!

In a growing relationship with Christ, these virtues should become a regular part of our everyday lives. If we learn to apply them to the deepest and darkest corners of our beings, things like jealousy will not be able to survive within us.

Getting to the Roots

The best thing about a "Galatians 5" approach to life is that, unlike jealousy, it puts our focus precisely where it needs to be. By applying the fruit of the Spirit to our relationships, we take care of the *roots* of our problems.

Jealousy does the exact opposite.

By allowing ourselves to be jealous of others, we avoid having to deal with our true problems. We ignore our insecurities, our "inadequacies," and our "areas of incompetence." We blame other people for our feelings of misery: It's all their fault! If only they weren't quite so wonderful, then we wouldn't feel so bad around them, right?

Well, not really.

The *truth* is that jealousy usually takes the place of something that we are not willing to accept about ourselves. In the case of my sister and me, for example, I was not secure with my own appearance, my own sense of humor, or my own dating status. I thought that I wasn't pretty enough, funny enough, or likable enough. Instead of taking care of those personal issues as I should have, I dumped them all on my sister in the form of jealousy.

To make matters worse, my jealousy eventually became a thick wall between Sarah and me. Because I viewed her as a hazard to my self-esteem, I became convinced that there wasn't much to her that was worth liking or even getting to know. I didn't see that a relationship with my own sister could be worth having, so I blocked myself off from her almost completely.

This is not the type of life that God wants for His children.

Jealousy does not make us feel any better about ourselves. It does not prevent a single negative opinion that we can have. And trust me, jealousy cannot make us feel any prettier, funnier, more likable, or whatever else we want to be. It is a means to escape our insecurities—nothing more.

Sometimes it's just *so easy* to fall into being jealous. Yet God has victory for us in this area.

A Test

On the night of Sarah's first date, for example, I was *so tempted* to be jealous of her. She left in a flurry of excitement, with a huge smile on her face, delight showing in her eyes, and a handsome boy on her arm. I went to my room and cried—alone—for a long time.

The insecurities that I thought I had dealt with seemed to be flooding over me once again. *I* wanted to be dating somebody, but instead, my little sister got to.

In days before I would have allowed myself to blame Sarah for the pain I experienced that night, but I did not want to be a slave to jealousy again. Instead, I prayed through tears for strength to get past my hurts so that there could be peace in my own life, dateless as it was.

When my sister arrived home hours later, God had brought me to the point where I could separate the fact that she was dating from the fact that I felt lonely. So despite my wounded spirit, I put a smile on my face and boldly crossed the ten feet that separated her bedroom from mine. I cleared my throat so she would notice me standing in her doorway. Then came a milestone in my life.

"How'd it go?" I asked.

She looked at me and smiled, and I knew instantly that a small battle in my war against jealousy had been won.

After the Fact

Through time my relationship with Sarah has grown incredibly. I now think of her not only as my beautiful, funny, and talented little sister but also as my closest friend. In fact, I'm hoping that someday she'll stand right next to me at my wedding.

When I look back over my life as a big sister, I can't believe how close I came to letting jealousy win—how close I came to letting my sister remain nothing more than "That Girl" in my life. And so I ask: How are you treating "That Girl" in yours?

- That girl whom it is so easy to be jealous of?
- That girl whom you want so much to dislike?
- That girl who seems to be the single reason for your misery?
- That girl who (could it be true?) hasn't really done anything wrong at all?

Could you be missing out on companionship with someone because you have let jealousy get between the two of you? Have you built up walls that prevent relationships from even happening? If so, take it from a girl who almost missed out on a friendship with her own sister: Jealousy just isn't worth it.

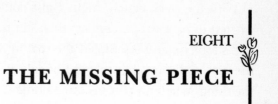

EIGHT

THE MISSING PIECE

Like a city whose walls are broken down is a man who
lacks self-control.

PROVERBS 25:28

My parents had always talked about wanting a park bench for their flower garden, so when my siblings and I saw one on sale, we bought it immediately. It was December at the time, and we planned to give the seat to our parents for their anniversary, even though that date wasn't until August. Our intentions were to hide the bench for eight months and then wrap it up nicely and give it to our parents in the summer.

That was the plan, at least. But the problem with our plan was that *I* had been put in charge of hiding the bench.

Now, before I go on with my story, I must explain here that I absolutely adore presents. Nothing in the world can make me smile like seeing a Christmas tree with stacks of pretty boxes and bags underneath it. Birthdays are some of my favorite days of the whole year, all because of presents.

I love shopping for presents, packaging presents, and receiving presents. What I especially love, though, is giving presents.

With the park bench, then, I just couldn't wait. I was so excited to have my parents see their gift that I pulled out my dad's toolbox and assembled the seat in our living room on the very night my siblings and I bought it. I didn't even wrap the thing. When my parents came home that evening, there it was, eight months early.

Did I mention how much I love presents?

Sadly, the park bench incident wasn't the only one of its kind. Once, for my mom's birthday, we bought her a straw hat two weeks early, and again my siblings trusted me to hide it. (You'd think they would learn.) That time I "accidentally" left the hat on our mom's bed so she would see it when she got home from work.

Needless to say, my siblings were never very happy with the fact that I liked to give presents prematurely. (To this day, whenever they want to insult me, they start talking about straw hats and park benches.) They always told me that I had ruined the presents, that it wasn't nearly as fun to open gifts before the proper day.

It wasn't until recently that I started to believe them.

A Few Days Early

It was during the first month of my freshman year at college that I experienced my nineteenth birthday, the first birthday I had ever had away from home. Several days before the big day, my family sent me a large box that was covered all over with these words:

DO NOT OPEN UNTIL SEPTEMBER 17!

I couldn't decide if this was a threat, a warning, or simply words of advice. Regardless, I stashed the box under my bed for a while, taking it out every hour or so to jiggle it and figure out what sounds its contents made. With every shake I grew more impatient to open my present.

Two days before my birthday, I just couldn't take the suspense any longer. No matter how much I tried to ignore the box, I couldn't put its mocking presence out of my mind. Whenever I was in my room, it taunted me!

Since my family wasn't there to police the situation or tie me down, I was able to be just as rebellious as I wanted to be. I tore through the wrapping, completely disregarding all of the "Do not open ..." warnings on it. With a sigh of relief, I pulled the lid off the box and checked out every single gift inside, admiring each one in turn.

But minutes later, with the contents of my birthday box strewn all over my bed, disappointment set in. I was amazed at how quickly it came on me. As soon as I had taken the lid off of my box, I was forced to accept the fact that there would be nothing for me to open on my birthday.

I had given myself no alternative. There would be no bows to untie, no paper to rip, on the day I actually turned nineteen. Although I had loathed being forced to wait, I really missed the waiting and anticipation when it was over. As much as I hated to admit it, the waiting and wondering were what made my birthday box so great.

So when the last of my presents had been tried out and tried on, I found myself wishing that I had saved something, at least one thing. Maybe even everything.

To Learn or Not to Learn

It's funny, isn't it? No matter how many times people try to teach us something, we usually have to learn our lessons the hard way in order to have them really sink in. Regardless of how many times my family told me that I should *wait* and give birthday gifts on birthdays and anniversary gifts on anniversaries, I didn't believe them until I had ruined one of my own special days.

Similar to my birthday box lesson, there have been numerous bits of wisdom that I have had to learn the hard way. Some, as with the bench and the hat, have been silly and mostly harmless. Some have been more serious. But they have all been learned as a result of my moments of ignorance, stupidity, or just plain stubbornness.

But as I keep learning how to "step back" in life, I am discovering more and more that many lessons are good *not* to learn through personal experience. As my friend Dan Seaborn points out, a *smart* person learns from his own mistakes, but a truly *wise* person can learn from the mistakes of others.[1]

I don't want to learn the most difficult lessons the hard way. I want to avoid making huge mistakes and poor decisions, things that I could regret for many years to come.

And as I observe other people around me, especially other women, I can't help but pick out one particular mistake that I really don't want to make.

Almost Perfect

After a whole year of planning, Valerie's day finally had come. She stood in front of the full-length mirror and smiled wider than she had ever smiled before. Her hair had been done up in loose curls, and her long white gown fit beautifully. Her face sparkled, and her eyes shone with excitement and anticipation.

In a matter of hours, Valerie would marry Brian, her prince.

The wedding ceremony had been planned with great care and great style, down to the slightest detail. The little church on the corner was filled with roses and bows for the special occasion. Bouquets were bunched, a lace runner stood waiting to be rolled up the aisle, and rice was on hand for the couple's exit. A photographer was already snapping pictures.

In the reception hall centerpieces graced the tables, and caterers were preparing enormous amounts of delicious food. Gifts were stacked in one corner, and a guest book lay open in the foyer. A getaway car was stowed back behind the church.

The vows were written. Everything was ready to go.

And then the moment arrived. With a booming crescendo from the sanctuary, two doors in front of Valerie swung open, and she made her entrance—*the* entrance. On her father's arm and with her friends rising to greet her, she looked straight ahead, straight at Brian.

Half an hour later Valerie walked down that same aisle, Brian's wife at last. Guests clapped as the couple passed.

Then, almost before the bride and groom had exited the sanctuary, people began whispering about how wonderful a wedding it had been. The flowers were lovely, the songs ideal, and the candlewicks had caught fire without any problems at all. Indeed, the ceremony had gone off without a hitch (except for the screaming ring bearer, of course). Everything seemed perfect.

But *everything* wasn't perfect. Something was missing.

An Amazing Girl

The very first time that Brian saw Valerie was four years earlier, before a chapel service during the first week of his freshman year at college. He and his friend Joel were sitting together in the chapel auditorium, watching other people enter the place. (Actually, they were watching *girls* enter the place.)

That was when Valerie walked in—and Brian's full attention was stolen for life. From across the room he watched in a trance as her long blonde hair bounced its way toward a seat. Then, without losing sight of her and without a moment's hesitation, he turned to his friend Joel.

Nodding in Valerie's direction, Brian asked, "Do you see that girl, the blonde one?"

Joel looked, raised his eyebrows, and nodded slowly. Then, as both guys stared at Valerie, Brian spoke the words that started it all.

"Mark my words, Joel," he said, "before my four years are up here, I'm going to ask *that* girl out."

It's really no surprise that Valerie caught Brian's eye the way she did. She seemed to have that effect on lots of people.

Valerie had always been that one special girl in her class who stood out more than all the others did. Her blonde hair was long and shiny, and she had deep blue eyes—eyes that made people stop and take a second look.

Valerie was beautiful in a spectacular sort of way, but she didn't act like most spectacularly beautiful people act. She loved hugs, and she loved the color pink. Her face lit up whenever she saw a friend, and Valerie was a friend to *everybody*. She had a ringing laugh that could bring smiles to just about any face, and she had an uncommon way of making even the heaviest situation a little bit lighter. She really was quite amazing.

Deep Regrets

Of course, Brian did work up the nerve to follow through on his promise to ask Valerie out. And when he did, everything clicked between the two of them. Their personalities were a great match, they had similar dreams, and they both wanted to honor God in their relationships.

While they were dating, then, Brian and Valerie were both committed to sexual purity in their relationship. They wanted to save sex for marriage, so they waited for each other. And four years after they had met, when they said, "I do," in the little church on the corner, Brian and Valerie had never slept together.

Still, there was that one missing piece. You see, Brian had waited his whole life for Valerie alone. Although Valerie had waited to have sex with her husband, Valerie had already lost her virginity.

It had happened during high school, long before Valerie became a Christian and long before Brian laid eyes on her. It had happened with a guy whom Valerie had loved at the time, but that guy was no longer a part of her life.

It had happened, and Valerie deeply regretted it. She regretted it because she knew it was wrong. She regretted it because it had stolen something from her husband. And she regretted it because she would have to live with it for the rest of her life.

Nothing Left

I wish I could tell you that Valerie's story is the only one of its kind that I have heard, but I can't. I have watched many friends and loved ones grieve a premature loss of virginity. And while I don't enjoy rehashing their guilt and pain, I think that it's important for us to be aware of their stories.

Abby was a newly married young woman when I met her, and one of our earliest conversations was about sex. Abby told me that during her early adulthood, she had been sexually active with a number of men. Many she knew well; many she hardly knew at all. For quite some time this went on, until Abby had a traumatic experience that made her rethink her lifestyle and her priorities.

Abby made a commitment to Christ and a commitment to stop having sex until she was married. With God's grace she stuck to both commitments. But even despite that fact, she carried deep regrets into her marriage.

She had shared intimate pieces of herself with so many men that she had a hard time forgetting them all and a hard time forgiving herself. She wished that she could go back and erase the relationships and experiences in her past, but she couldn't.

Worst of all, though, Abby had forever lost the gift of her virginity, a gift that she wished she had saved for her husband. "I didn't have anything left to give to just *him*," she told me, with tears streaming down her cheeks.

A few months ago I received a letter from another young woman, a close friend:

> I have failed with regard to sexual purity, and the man I am preparing to marry has made no mistakes in that area. (I was the first girl to hold his hand and the first girl he ever kissed.) Because of my mistakes, I have had to watch him mourn the loss of my purity, a gift that might have been his. I have had to answer hard questions about my choices, and while I believe that God can work my mistakes for the good of His kingdom, I cannot help but weep for the pain I have caused those I love.

If you could have the chance to talk to any of these people today, they would most certainly warn you against having sex before marriage. They would ask you to learn from their mistakes rather than making the same mistakes on your own. They would tell you how much they still hurt inside, and they would advise you to avoid such a hurt at all costs.

The more I listen to the people around me, the more I am persuaded that I don't ever want to experience the type of pain that stems from lost innocence. After having far too many tear-filled conversations with friends and loved ones, I am convinced that the loss of one's physical virginity is not just a momentary thing.

The loss of one's virginity has the potential to reach far into the future, affecting lives months and even years after it happens. It can upset the core of a person's identity, and it can wreak havoc on one's self-esteem. For many people it is the root of guilt, unhappiness, and even depression.

Worst of all, though, sexual sin puts up walls between people and their Creator. As one young woman said, "Sexual impurity makes you feel distant from God."

Warning Labels

In the very first chapter of the very first book of the Bible, God commanded humanity to "be fruitful and increase in number" (Genesis 1:28). From the beginning of time, His plan was that two people—one man and one woman—would "become one flesh" (Genesis 2:24) and reproduce. And when God told humans to do this, He (true to form) made it interesting. Instead of handing us a set of "baby assembly instructions," He gave us the gift of sex, the most intimate of all physical acts.

And not only did God create sex for humans, but He also created humans for sex. He gave us the desire to reproduce and the desire to experience physical intimacy with the opposite sex. He filled us with a special supply of chemicals and hormones and brain synapses (and a whole bunch of other things that are really hard to pronounce) that work just for sexual intercourse. Isn't that amazing?

God created sex for humans and humans for sex. That's the beauty of it. That's also the problem.

Although God created humans to have sex, He also told

them to wait for it. Throughout the Bible there are instances when God's followers were instructed in their physical relationships.

One of the Ten Commandments is "You shall not commit adultery" (Exodus 20:14). The Book of Leviticus details many specific laws concerning sexual union.

In the New Testament the guidelines continue. Paul wrote that "the body is not meant for sexual immorality" (1 Corinthians 6:13) and that "he who sins sexually sins against his own body ... [God's] temple" (1 Corinthians 6:18-19). The Book of Hebrews says that the "marriage bed [should be] kept pure" (13:4), and Jesus Himself said that sexual sin was one of the things that made a person "unclean" (Matthew 15:19-20).

Now, to many people, these biblical guidelines may seem to completely contradict the fact that God created humans for sexual intercourse. "If sex is such a great gift," they ask, "then why does God tell us we can't have it?"

Good question.

Here's an answer: God *doesn't* tell us that we can't have sex. He tells us that we *can*. He simply tells us *when* we can have it.

God is not in the business of spiteful withholding. He doesn't deny His people good gifts unless He has a good reason to do so. Similar to how a child's toy usually has a cautionary sticker on it somewhere, God attached a "warning label" of sorts to sex.

Although God created sex to be fun and cool and exciting for His people, He also understood that sex under certain circumstances could be very damaging. He knew that intercourse outside of a marriage relationship would be the root of deep pain for people like Valerie, Abby, and countless others.

And so, in His infinite wisdom, God told His people to wait for sex.

Maximum Sex

My friend Jamie and her husband Mike recently got married, and both of them were virgins when they said, "I do." I asked Jamie's about the rewards of waiting for sex, and her response was so great that I thought I would share it here.

"You can't understand how glad we are that we waited for each other," she said. "There are no diseases to worry about, and I don't have to worry about how I rate compared to someone from his past. It is freedom."

Now, please, allow me to gush for a moment.

Can you imagine how great it would feel to know that someone had waited his whole life for you alone? Can you imagine how wonderful it would be to say that you had done the same for him? (I get goose bumps just thinking about it!) It would be so special, so intimate, so meaningful.

Friends, *that* is why God tells us to wait. He wants us to experience the best kind of physical intimacy there is ("maximum sex," as a pastor at my church once called it). God offers each of us the best version of sex that we could possibly receive: sex within the confines of a trusting and committed relationship.

I hope with all my heart that someday I'll get to experience a physical relationship like the one my friend Jamie has:

- sex without the anxiety that my partner will dump me the next morning;
- sex without the fear of catching a disease;

- sex combined with a deep, unselfish, and lasting love;
- sex with a person who loved me before sex; and
- sex with a person who loved me enough to wait.

Getting Personal

If you are one of the fortunate people whose virginity is still intact, rejoice! You have a precious gift, a priceless gift. Cherish it. Guard it. Know that there are many who wish they still had what you have, and be wise enough to learn from their mistakes.

Most importantly, though, remember what 1 Corinthians 10:12 says: "If you think you are standing firm, be careful that you don't fall!" Be sure to read chapter nine for more guidance on maintaining your purity.

Now, if you are a person who has lost your innocence prematurely, I apologize if this chapter has been difficult to read. (It gets easier from this point on.) Know that in Christ there is still hope.

Like all other times that we sin against God, when we have sex outside of marriage, we can still find forgiveness. Through God's grace toward us and because of Jesus Christ's death *in our place,* even this sin has been accounted for. The Bible says that if we will confess our sins to God, He is faithful enough to forgive us of *all* our unrighteousness (see 1 John 1:9). Through such forgiveness we can go on as new creations in Him, people who have been made whole again.

When Jesus walked the earth, He often surprised His followers by hanging out with a seemingly tough crowd. Many of the people whom He spent time with had colored pasts, to say the least. He hung out with tax collectors, prostitutes, contagiously sick people, and Roman soldiers.

These people were the ones who seemed to be the most distant from God, but they were also the ones whom Jesus reached out to most often. He saw their sin, and He saw *through* their sin enough to forgive them.

You may feel that you have already failed completely in the area of sexual purity. You may feel that there is no way to ever recapture the innocence that you once had. You may feel as if there's no hope that you'll ever feel whole again. You may feel that you have cheated your future mate of a gift that should have been his. You may feel that you should have done a lot of things differently.

No matter what your story is, no matter what things seem to scar your past, there is hope for a future that is pure and clean. In Christ there is forgiveness for all our bad choices. In Christ you can say what King David said long ago: "Then I acknowledged my sin to you and did not cover up my iniquity. I said, 'I will confess my transgressions to the Lord'—and you forgave the guilt of my sin" (Psalm 32:5).

If you need to be forgiven of sexual sin, take some time right now and ask God for His forgiveness. He'll give it (I promise!). Put this book down for however long it takes, and come back when you're finished.

A Step Further

OK, you've made a mistake, you've asked forgiveness, and you have been forgiven. Now there's just one more thing.

When we receive God's grace, it should make a difference in the way we live our lives. As Ephesians 4:24 says, we should "put on the new self, created to be like God in true righteousness and holiness."

True guilt includes the desire to never feel such guilt again. In the same way, true repentance implies a major shift in behavior. If we truly regret making a mistake once, we will try hard not to make the same mistake again. As Proverbs 26:11 says, "As a dog returns to its vomit, so a fool repeats his folly."

After we've received forgiveness for a specific sin once, we should find ways to avoid that sin in the future. "We died to sin," says Romans 6:2. "How can we live in it any longer?"

We should begin to live differently than before, taking steps to make obedience a more natural part of our lives. We should avoid the types of situations that led to our former shortfalls. We should find people to help us make the correct decisions, and we should avoid people who encourage poor choices—at least until we can stand firmly on our own.

Now, does this mean that we won't *ever* make the same mistake twice? Not necessarily. We might need to ask forgiveness again, but our aim should always be to get better at obedience. C.S. Lewis, a famous Christian writer, put it this way:

> We may, indeed, be sure that perfect chastity ... will not be attained by any merely human efforts. You must ask for God's help. Even when you have done so, it may seem

to you for a long time that no help, or less help than you need, is being given. Never mind. After each failure, ask forgiveness, pick yourself up, and try again. Very often what God first helps us towards is not the virtue itself but just this power of always trying again.[2]

No matter what your level of sexual experience is today, God offers you a future that is full and clean. You can start again. (Read chapter nine for some ideas on where to start.)

As Martha Bolton writes, "When a mountain climber slips and slides down a few feet, he doesn't give up and walk down the rest of the mountain defeated. He just keeps right on climbing, only now he knows where not to place his foot."[3]

NINE

PURPLE STUFF AND
OTHER EXTRAS

She brings him good, not harm, all the days of her life.
PROVERBS 31:12

It was a church youth service of all places, and I was sitting next to "Jeff," a guy on whom I had a big crush at the time. Jeff and I were attending the service with a whole group of friends, but the two of us just happened to be sitting right next to each other on that particular night.

Imagine that.

The place was packed, so our folding chairs had been set up fairly close together. Needless to say, Jeff and I were sitting fairly close together, too. I couldn't have asked for a better scenario. Everything seemed to be going perfectly. I reveled in my strategic seat-picking skills and kept hoping that people thought Jeff and I were *together*. In fact, I spent much of the service thinking about how cute we must have looked sitting side by side.

But then something happened that changed the entire night for me. Halfway through the minister's talk, Jeff shifted positions, and his pant leg brushed ever so slightly against mine. The contact was so subtle that I'm not sure if he even noticed it.

But *I* certainly did.

Lightning-fast, my brain switched gears, and tingles shot all the way from my knees to my toes. A blush rushed to my cheeks, and for a moment, time stopped. Over and over, a single thought was racing through my head: *Well, this is nice.*

I stared into space for a few seconds and then sucked in a quick breath of air. Shaking my head, I scrambled to erase the glazed-over look from my eyes, to regain some of my composure.

Stop thinking what you're thinking, Lisa!

A few more seconds passed, and I tried again.

Seriously, stop it!

A few more seconds.

Stop it, stop it, stop it!

And a few more seconds passed.

Four Rows From the Front

I used to think that sexual purity was an uncomplicated issue. I thought that I could breeze right through my life without ever struggling over issues of physical intimacy. I thought that abstinence would be easy.

When I was growing up, I attended youth conferences all over the place and heard speakers talk about things like kisses and virginity and holding hands. On occasion the speakers would even share some juicy details from their own personal lives. Usually, though, they kept things to a pretty familiar script: "Save your sexual purity!" they would say. "Put your future mate's name on top of it, and don't give it to anyone else!"

My response to such speeches was always the same. Sitting in my seat (always four rows from the front), I would nod my head, agreeing that abstinence was the best way to go in life. I would smile my way through Bible verses about self-control, and I would stand up with confidence when the speaker asked me to save my virginity for my husband and for my wedding night. Without hesitation, I would sign another pledge card.

A few years have passed since my youth conference days, and a few things have changed over that period of time. I sit eight or ten rows from the front now, and I don't have many chances to sign pledge cards anymore. It is a rare occasion when I hear a speaker discuss sexual purity, and it has been a long time since I've heard *any* juicy details shared from the pulpit.

All of those things have changed considerably, but they don't really matter much. What matters is that my attitude toward sexual purity has changed. It has changed on a drastic scale.

Back when I made my youth conference commitments, they weren't empty promises by any means. I fully intended to hold myself to them all. I had set my mind on preserving my virginity, and I planned to live a life of abstinence until I became a married woman. I made my vows, I made them firmly, and I anticipated keeping them. Even so, I didn't really understand what types of things my commitments would involve.

Years after my pledge cards were collected, I have finally begun to grasp some of the depth and difficulty in the vows that I made.

So today, when I am given the chance to commit to abstinence, I still stand up with confidence—but I pause and take a deep breath first. When I am asked to put my signature on the dotted line, I still willingly sign—but my pen moves a little more deliberately than it used to.

And when those familiar Bible verses get quoted, I don't nod my head anymore. I set my jaw.

As the Dominoes Fall

C.S. Lewis once said that "chastity is the most unpopular of the Christian virtues."[1] I think I'm beginning to understand why he said that. It's really hard to guard your purity sometimes!

Now, I'm not about to pretend that I know everything there is to know about sexual purity. I *don't* understand it all. In fact, I'll readily admit that I am quite the novice when it comes to physical relationships. How could I not be, with all that confetti in my closet?

Still, even *I* know that sexual purity is not easy. (If you haven't figured this one out for yourself yet, let me clue you in.) No matter how spiritual or how religious we are, part of what makes us human is that we get enticed by the idea of sex. Once we hit puberty, it just comes with the territory. Whether we're in committed relationships or not, certain physical temptations exist for all of us.

The slightest touch—even the most innocent and friendly type of contact—can send our brains whirling in the wrong direction. It can take only a moment for everything to get all jumbled up and swirled around in our heads. In no time at all our thoughts can be consumed with desire. These temptations are real, they're strong, and they're not going to get any weaker. (We'll discuss this more later.)

Besides the issue of temptation, the really tough thing about sexual purity (or "physical intimacy" as some call it) is that there are tons of levels to it. It's much more than just *intercourse*. From the almost impersonal to the incredibly intimate, there are various steps that take place before sex in a physical relationship. And although it may seem unnecessary to list these steps, I think it really helps our understanding of purity to do so.

Since I don't have much personal experience on this subject, I've borrowed a list from a woman named Dannah Gresh. (She's married, so we can be pretty confident that she knows what she's talking about.) In her book *And The Bride Wore White*, Dannah says that there are nine basic "Steps to Physical Intimacy." Here's how she describes them:

1. making eye contact
2. talking to a guy
3. holding hands
4. putting hands on shoulders and hands on waist
5. kissing on the cheek or softly kissing on the lips
6. open-mouthed, passionate kissing
7. petting while clothed
8. "experimental" nakedness
9. sexual intercourse[2]

That seems easy enough, doesn't it? Yeah, sure, but the issue here is that these nine steps are not really "steps" at all.

Sexual purity is like a whole bunch of little dominoes lined up in a row. Each piece is connected and related to the other pieces, because they're all a part of the same chain. As one domino falls, it heads for another, and on and on down the line. Each early piece naturally progresses toward a later piece, and the later pieces do not normally fall until after the earlier ones have.

In a discussion about sex, then, it's not fair to jump straight to the final domino (intercourse), disregarding all of the other little pieces that lead right up to it. Without some of those earlier steps in a physical relationship, it's doubtful that sex would happen. If we step back and look at the big picture of sexual purity, we'll see that *every* physical milestone is an integral part of the chain. Each one matters.

A Midnight Confession

It was very late one evening when I heard a slight "tap, tapping" on my dorm room door. Surprised, I laid my homework aside and went over to see who was there. My friend Emma greeted me with a small smile, but the lines on her face and the slumping of her shoulders told me that something big was bothering her.

Emma entered my room and took a seat cross-legged on my bed. I sat down, facing her, and then became quiet, waiting for her to say what was on her mind.

"You've probably wondered," she began, "about Jared and me."

I nodded and didn't say anything. I *had* wondered about the two of them. From what I could tell, the relationship they shared was extremely complicated. The two of them dated each other on and off, breaking up and getting back together and breaking up and getting back together. For the life of me, I could never figure out if Jared and Emma were boyfriend and girlfriend or "just friends."

My gut instinct told me that something about the relationship was really weird. No matter how many times they tried, they couldn't find a way to make romance work for them. Their on-again, off-again cycle kept on going—right up to the moment when Emma sat on my bed with her feet tucked beneath her knees.

After an hour-long conversation with my friend, the doubts in my head made much more sense. Emma told me some of the details about her relationship with Jared. Certain parts of her story were fun and sweet, events like their first kiss and remembrances of the little ways they had been affectionate toward each other. But the sweet things were not what had brought Emma to my door.

Emma had let the physical part of her relationship with Jared go much farther than she felt it should have. "We never had sex," she explained, "but we did almost everything else."

Emma deeply regretted crossing the lines that she had crossed with Jared. She had repeatedly done things that she wished she hadn't. Even though she was still a virgin, Emma had given away intimate pieces of herself, pieces that she really wanted to take back. With a tight and choked-up voice, she tried to express the fullness of her hurts: "I feel so sorry for the things that were lost."

As Emma discovered far too late, sex isn't the only piece in this chain of physical intimacy that matters. In the same way, sex isn't the only action that can be accompanied by feelings of guilt or remorse.

Different Levels, Same Lesson

When I first started writing this book, I began asking young women I knew if they had any regrets in the area of sexual purity. As I expected, their levels of physical experience varied. Some of the women had only kissed a guy, some had already lost their virginity, and some told me they fell in between those two groups.

Now, I wasn't surprised to find out that the women I interviewed had experienced different levels of intimacy. I expected that. I *was* surprised, though, to find that almost *all* the women I talked to either had felt or were still feeling regret over the physical intimacy they had experienced.

A young woman named Alexis told me that she had never had sex, but she thought that she and a guy went "way too far" one night. At the time I spoke to Alexis, the memories that she carried from that single evening still played over and over in her head, and she didn't know how to get rid of them. She told me that she hated remembering the things that *did* happen that night and even felt haunted by the thought of what *could have* happened.

It didn't surprise me to hear that people like Alexis—people who had experienced a high level of physical intimacy—felt regret over their actions. I had always assumed that those who had "gone further" physically would carry more regret than those who hadn't gone as far. A woman who had lost her virginity would naturally feel much more remorse than someone who had only kissed a guy, right?

Not always. As I was shocked to discover, many women regret entering even the earliest stages of physical intimacy. Whether this involved soft kisses or just holding hands, the overall theme was easily apparent: "I can't believe I let that scumbag touch me."

A young woman named Chelsea told me that she had repeatedly given her kisses away to guys who didn't deserve them. Andrea shared a similar testimony: "I honestly regret every kiss that I've ever had. When I think about my future husband, it makes me want to go back in time and take all of them back."

Although the women I interviewed had experienced very different levels of intimacy, almost all of them shared the same type of regret. With few exceptions, each person had learned to cherish something, but each one had learned too late.

Un-Regrettable

It has been said that the passion in a kiss is what gives it its sweetness, that the affection in a kiss is what sanctifies it.[3] Now, the word *passion* has several meanings, not all of them healthy. But if we define it here as "deep and sincere love," as I think the original speaker intended, I love that saying for two reasons.

First, I love it because I think it's true. Second, I love it because I think it sheds light on a much bigger concept than just kissing. In fact, I think it can help to explain why people can regret even seemingly innocent acts of intimacy.

Because of a whole lot of fun emotions, our physical expressions of love are much more than just *physical* actions. For example, when a kiss has love to back it up, it becomes much more than just two pairs of lips hanging out for a while. If the holding of hands is accompanied by deep affection, the connection isn't merely between interlocking fingers.

The reason why sex isn't the only thing that can lead to regret is because *all* physical intimacy involves more than just human bodies. *All* physical intimacy has feeling and emotion woven through it. And because of this, *all* physical intimacy has the ability to affect a person's emotional identity.

Now, kissing somebody will most likely *not* lead to the same level of regret that sexual intercourse will lead to. That goes without saying, but that's not the point here. The point is that even seemingly innocent expressions of love can be sources of regret later on.

I don't know about you, but I would like to avoid as much regret as I possibly can. And as my friend Mandy once said, "Regret is not something that you necessarily *have* to feel." You don't *have* to feel shame when you look back on your history of physical intimacy. You don't *have* to feel guilty for what you did with which guy and when you did it. You don't *have* to feel sorry for the way you showed your love to the opposite sex.

Trust me, you don't *have* to. But there's a catch, you see, because a life of no regrets doesn't just happen.

If you don't want to deal with things like guilt, shame, and disappointment later on in life, then you'll have to start *now* by making choices that won't result in those things. In the same way that tomorrow's harvest depends on today's planting season, tomorrow's regret depends on today's decisions. If you don't want to regret your physical intimacy tomorrow, then you'll have to be living in un-regrettable physical intimacy today.

A Step Back

Remember the whole "domino analogy" from a few pages ago? (Hint: The levels of physical intimacy are like dominoes all lined up in a row.) Let's get back to that for a second, OK? Because the easiest way to avoid regret in the area of sexual purity is to learn *how* and *where* to stop those dominoes from falling.

Recently there has been a lot of discussion among Christians about this issue of "stopping the dominoes." Practically every day somebody else comes out with a new book on what things are OK to do, with whom it's OK to do them, and when it's OK to do them with the previously mentioned "whom." It is not my intent to add yet another voice to that already overwhelming racket.

That said, I *would* like to offer some suggestions with the hope that they will help you come to your own conclusions on this matter of "dominoes." Let's chat for a bit, OK? Come on, I promise not to say that you can't kiss a boy.

The Big Picture

When I initially started planning my First Kiss Party, I was absolutely thrilled by the daydreaming that it made me do.

After every trip to the party supply store, I would sit in my room and sort through my stash. All the while my mind swirled with excitement as I envisioned the future.

I wonder how long it will be until I open this stuff, I often thought. *Surely it can't be much further away.* With that very idea, my imagination went into full gear, picturing the scene. *One of these days IT will happen,* I told myself, *a kiss to make the stars dance.*

As months passed and my party stash grew, my "first kiss dreams" became bigger and bigger. Over time I imagined practically every scenario there was to imagine: from the normal and everyday events (during a movie, after a date, on a walk) to the typical girly stuff (after a poem, during a serenade, in a moonlit gazebo) to the over-the-top and completely extravagant (on a roller coaster, on TV, in front of hundreds of people ...). You get the picture.

As my imaginings got more and more spectacular, I was surprised by the way they affected me. Oh, sure, each time I pictured my first kiss under a starry sky, it was exciting, really exciting. But it was also very saddening, because I realized that I would only get to give away that first kiss *once.* Someday (*please, Lord*) it would happen. And then it would be over.

It would be *over.*

The thought alone produced a lump of emotion in my throat. I began to view this issue of physical intimacy differently than I had before. I stopped thinking about my romantic "firsts" in terms of things to scratch off a personal "To Do" list. Instead, I started to see some of the value and the preciousness that each one held.

I could no longer view my first kiss (or my first *anything,* for that matter) as just another roadblock on the way to "happily ever after." No, due to all my dreaming, that first kiss had transformed into something entirely different:

An individual slice of time.

An eternal milestone on my Road of Life.

A future memory that could happen only once.

Something worth cherishing.

The Big Question

In most discussions about sexual purity, it's almost certain that at least one person will ask something like this: "How far can I go before marriage?"

In an instant, ten different people will launch into detailed descriptions of their ten shockingly different convictions. Each person quotes a verse or two of Scripture, and each person argues a solid case for his or her own principles. In the end, though, we're left with more questions than we had in the beginning:

Can I do everything *as long as I don't have sexual intercourse? What about oral sex? Am I being impure if I kiss somebody before I'm married? Should I avoid holding hands?*

And so the debate gets deeper and more heated and more confusing—to the point where people throw up their hands in defeat and leave without a solid grasp on purity, without an answer to that one single question that keeps on burning, stronger than ever: "How far *can* I go?"

Have you ever pondered that question? I have. In fact, after having asked myself that question over and over and over again, I'll let you in on a little secret: *That* question doesn't have a good answer.

Oh, sure, there are answers to the "How far ..." question that make sense to an intelligent brain. There are answers to the "How far ..." question that will help a person avoid regret. There are answers to the "How far ..." question that align with God's Word, too. Even so, the answers that we'll come across by asking ourselves, "How far can I go?" are not the best of all answers—and I'll tell you why.

With all due respect, we've been asking ourselves the wrong question.

No Place for Daredevils

If a woman wanted to avoid falling off a cliff, she wouldn't attempt cartwheels along the edge, would she? She wouldn't walk right up to the side of the rock and do a little dance, either. She wouldn't dangle one foot off the overhang. That's the kind of stuff we leave to highly paid super stuntwomen with harnesses and huge insurance policies.

No, if a wise woman wanted to avoid falling off a cliff, she would find ways to keep herself away from the ledge. She would maintain a safe distance from the danger of the rock, no matter how much she wanted to experience its thrills. She might even put up a fence between herself and the overhang. That way she could do all the cartwheels she wanted without any risk of falling.

Friends, this is exactly why "How far can I go?" is *not* the question to ask when we're seeking to live in sexual purity.

"How far ...?" brings us right up to the very edge of sexual sin—so close that it only takes one misstep for all to be lost. "How far ...?" leads us too close to the danger that we say we're trying to avoid. "How far ...?" is a cartwheel on the ledge of sexual purity.

In his book *You Are Not Your Own,* singer Jason Perry discusses how he got to the point where he gave away his virginity. "I'd been laying the groundwork for a long time without even realizing it," he writes. "I had played ... to see how far I could go without actually having sex. It was a dangerous game, and it was fun. What I didn't realize, however, was that this game had no winners. I was gambling that I would be strong when the moment came. I lost the bet."[4]

As experience like Jason's proves, sexual purity is no place for daredevils. Walking along that ridge is a huge risk, and if we want to be pure, we would be wise to stay away from it. We would be wise to learn that asking, "How far can I go?" usually brings us much further than we really want to go. We would be wise to start asking ourselves a different question, a better question: "How much can I save?"

The Purple Stuff

A few years ago I had the opportunity to speak at a conference in sunny southern California. As I entered the church for the main rally, the first thing that caught my eye was the huge stash of door prizes on display on the platform. At least a hundred different items were sitting there, waiting for someone to win them.

What made the sight even greater was that each prize had been wrapped beautifully in sheer purple chiffon fabric, fastened with a purple ribbon, and labeled with a slip of purple paper to identify the donor of the prize.

I later learned that one woman had packaged all of the presents that I saw before me, devoting hours of her time to the project so that each gift would look nice for its recipient. She had cut every piece of fabric, hand-written all of the tags, and painstakingly tied bows on each of the gifts.

Her work had definitely paid off. The scene she had created could only be compared to Christmas (without the red and green, of course). Shiny ribbons caught the lights, and flowers and bows were everywhere. The purple stuff was absolutely perfect.

Now, in the same way that the wrapping paper, ribbons, and bows enhanced those presents, so can the gift of sex be enhanced. If intercourse is the gift that I am to save for my husband someday, then all those steps leading up to intercourse can be the wrapping around my gift, my very own "purple stuff."

Things like kisses, hugs, secret smiles, and shared dreams can be the wrapping on our gift of intimacy—the gift that can one day be presented in its entirety to the man of our dreams. With every new physical "first" that we give away, we're removing some of the splendor from that gift.

If we want to offer our mates the best gifts that we can possibly give them, we'll stop dangling our feet over the edges of cliffs. We'll stop asking, "How far can I go?" and start asking, "How much can I save?"

That's a Wrap

It's funny, when I'm focused on my own desires and my own wishes, it's hard for me to want to save my "purple stuff" for my mate. There are days when I really would like a good make-out session. But when I think about my future husband—even just the possibility that he's out there somewhere—all of that changes.

When I daydream about the moment that he'll look into my eyes, I feel a surge of excitement that doesn't compare to anything else. When I think about holding his hand for the rest of my life, I can't help but get all giddy inside. And when I imagine the first time he kisses me, my chest and my throat and my head begin to feel breezy.

And I remember that he'll be worth saving the purple stuff for.

The more I think about it, the more I know that I don't want to give away big parts of my sexual purity to someone who isn't willing to earn them. I don't want to waste my romantic "firsts" on a guy who won't stick around for me. I don't want to go to the very edge of my standards in a relationship that won't end up anywhere permanent.

And as my friend Julia says, "I want to offer my mate more than just a reproductive system." I want to save some "purple stuff" for him.

Getting Personal

My favorite Bible verse about this matter of *saving* appears in chapter eight of the Song of Songs. There a woman addresses her husband with this phrase: "Place me like a seal over your heart."[5] If I could speak with my future husband (*please, Lord*) at this very moment, I know that I would ask a similar thing of him. And I think he would ask a similar thing of me.

I want to honor God in the way that I use my body, and I want my mate to be the seal over my heart even before I meet him. So with those things in mind, I've done a lot of thinking about my purple stuff, and I've come to some conclusions that I'm happy with.

In an effort to keep myself from "falling off a cliff" someday, I've set up a few "fences" for myself in the area of physical intimacy. Here's what they are:

- I will save my kisses for the man I marry, and he can kiss me as soon as he puts an engagement ring on my finger.
- I will save everything past soft kisses for my wedding day.

That's simple enough, isn't it?

Now, I'm not about to say that these are the perfect fences, and I won't say that everyone else should build the exact same fences that I have built. What I will say, though, is that I am happy to strive for these standards, and I don't think I will ever regret them.

If you're wondering why I've decided to wait until (Lord willing) I get engaged to kiss, here is my explanation:

I don't think that there is anything wrong with soft kissing. Numerous people whom I trust and respect have told me that soft kissing is not "too far." This is why I don't feel the need to save kissing for marriage.

But I have decided to save my kisses for my engagement. I have a few relatively silly reasons. For example, "Since I've survived thus far without it, I figure I may as well wait for the man of my dreams." But my biggest reason to wait can be summed up in a great quote that Kathy, my editor, sent to me: "The decision to kiss for the first time is the most crucial in any love story. It changes the relationship of two people much more strongly than even the final surrender; because this kiss already has within it that surrender."[6]

My sentiments exactly, friends. (I only wish that *I* had been the one to say it.)

Now, if you're wondering why I've decided to wait for all the other stuff until (Lord willing again) I get married, here is my explanation:

I think that anything past soft kissing is entering into a whole new territory—a potentially dangerous territory. Dannah Gresh writes that "a new desire awakens" with passionate kisses. And frankly, I don't want to awaken that kind of desire until I can carry through with it. If this means that I don't get to experience any soap opera-type makin' out, for a while, so be it.

The Other Big Question

At this point I'm guessing that you've got at least one question for me in your head: *But won't it be too tempting to stop at such an early stage?*

Well, let's think about that for a second.

Considering the nature of humanity, sexual temptation either is or will be a given for all of us. And since our domino reactions begin with things like eye contact and innocent conversation, the desire for physical intimacy is not something that we can avoid—unless, of course, you can get by with never looking at or talking to a guy.

No matter where we build our fences, we'll be tempted to go farther. Still, the existence of temptation shouldn't change our response to it. As newlywed Bethany Torode writes:

> Passion begins the minute you glance into each other's eyes, and not kissing doesn't prevent it from building. Our wills, when in submission to the Holy Spirit, are strong enough to make sure that we will not compromise our principles. We can't blame blind passion when we fall short of our standards. We are never irrational to "the point of no return." We are not completely lost until we choose to lose ourselves.[7]

An often-quoted passage of the Bible (especially for the topic of sexual purity) is 1 Corinthians 10:13: "No temptation has seized you except what is common to man. And God is faithful; he will not let you be tempted beyond what you can bear. But when you are tempted, he will also provide a way out so that you can stand up under it."

Isn't that great? God wants to help us withstand temptation! He'll even give us a way out of the situation! (I don't know about you, but that makes me feel really good.)

In our thankfulness, though, let's not forget that God isn't the only piece to this puzzle. Yes, He *will* help us to manage tempting areas like sexual purity. Yes, He *will* provide a way out for us. Yes, yes—but He's certainly *not* going to do all of our work for us. God expects us to play our part, too.

Oftentimes the easiest *way out* of a tempting situation comes *way before* the temptation actually shows up. If you make a habit of lying around naked with a guy, don't expect saying "no" to sex to be easy. Don't think that a spiritual lightning bolt will come down and prevent you from having intercourse. That's insanity.

As 2 Peter 3:14 (NLT) says, we should "make every effort to live a pure and blameless life." And Paul says that we should "flee" from sexual sin (1 Corinthians 6:18). This is not merely a suggestion, friends; it's an expectation, a command. We should *run* from the sins that entice us, doing everything we possibly can do to avoid them.

A woman once told me that when she and her husband were still dating, there were times when she wouldn't even let him hold her hand because the temptation to go *too far* was *too strong*. If, like her, we can condition ourselves to choose purity in the small things, it will get easier and easier to be pure in the big things. If we learn how to stop at an early stage, we won't have to risk getting caught up in some later stages.

Sure, the choice is still there and the option remains the same. But when we're used to making the *right* choice, the right choice seems like the easier one.

Building Good Fences

The best way to achieve sexual purity is to stop kissing when we need to stop, stop hugging when we need to stop, and—recalling my "tingly toes" story at the beginning of this chapter—move our knees when we need to.

If you want to build some fences in your own life but you don't know how, here are a few things to consider:

1. **Listen to people who are older and more experienced than you are.** Ask people who are married (and people whom you respect) about what good fences look like. Tell them what you're up to, and ask them for some suggestions.
2. **Pray about it.** Ask God if He's OK with the fences that you're considering. Move your fences until He says "yes."
3. **Keep the "purple stuff" in mind.** Think about what kinds of things you would want your mate to save for *you*. Are you saving those things for him? (I moved a fence because of this one!)
4. **Decide *now.*** It might feel weird to set standards for things that seem a long way off, but when you're done, you'll be glad you did it.
5. **Be specific, even if it's awkward or embarrassing.** A weak fence doesn't do much good, so make sure your fences are built strong.
6. **Write your decisions down.** Write them in ink.
7. **Share your decisions with someone who will dare to ask you how you're doing.** I shared mine with my sister, because I know that she'll keep me accountable.

So now I ask: How easy has it been for you to choose purity? How easy are you making it for yourself? Have you set clear boundaries for your sexual purity from this point on? Or are you edging your way toward a cliff without any fences to keep you from falling off?

If you haven't built any personal fences yet, I would advise you to do so right away. You won't regret it! Your physical intimacy is yours alone to give, and it is also yours alone to save.

Put up some boundaries for yourself so that you can give your future mate a great present someday. And if you hit a rough patch, where temptation is especially strong, here's what I suggest: stop, pray, and remember how great it will be to offer your mate all of your love—*plus* some "purple stuff."

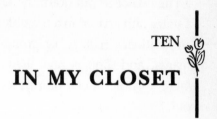

TEN

IN MY CLOSET

All my longings lie open before you, O Lord; my sighing is not hidden from you.

PSALM 38:9

I was getting ready to go to bed one snowy winter night at college when I heard a racket outside my window—chanting and running and cheering. Intrigued and slightly frightened, I pulled open the blinds and saw around forty or fifty young men running around my building, wearing only gym shorts and T-shirts.

What in the world is going on? I thought. *They must be crazy.*

I slid open my window so I could hear what the guys were saying, and a frigid gust of wind sliced right through me. I grabbed a sweater and tugged it on over my pajamas, all the while trying to figure out what the lunatics were yelling outside. After listening for a few seconds, I was able to make out these words: "COME DOWN OUT FRONT!"

Without another thought, I slammed my window shut and threw my hair into a ponytail. On the way out of my room, I nabbed one of my friends and told her to come with me. Whatever this was, it was something that we didn't want to miss.

The two of us ran down the hall, jumped down two flights of stairs, and arrived in a breathless frenzy at the main door to our residence hall. A big group of equally frenzied girls in pajamas and slippers had already gathered at the doorway, where a whole bunch of guys stood shivering outside in the cold.

As I observed the scene in front of me, one of the guys stepped out in front of all the others, lifted his hands, and counted to three. That was when the music started.

For the next ten minutes the women of Evans Hall were serenaded with a mix of cheesy love songs from the previous few decades. The guys sang all of their songs *a capella*, from "My Girl" to "You've Lost That Lovin' Feelin'." They had even incorporated some choreography into their little routine— dropping to a knee at one point and holding out roses during the final song.

I think I speak for every young woman present when I say that we were all on cloud nine. We smiled and giggled our way through the entire presentation.

When the last note had been sung, we ladies gave our chilled musicians a standing ovation and a chorus of rowdy cheers. Then, with icicles in our hair and newly warmed hearts, we shuffled off to bed and to a night of very sweet dreams.

Ah, boys are wonderful.

Quite a Wonder

I have two brothers, so I have long been acquainted with the fascination that males seem to find in sports, bugs, tools, and all things disgusting and smelly. I have personally marveled at how, no matter how old they are and no matter what the circumstances, they can always find something to mangle or destroy. And somehow they manage to keep their phone conversations to two-word questions and one-word responses.

Quite a wonder, indeed.

Despite all of their weird habits, though, I can't help but think that guys are absolutely adorable. It's so cute to see them hit each other on the backside during sports and slap each other during hugs. I love the fact that they get all nervous and uncomfortable when girls cry, and it's precious when they instinctively want to protect women.

So even though guys can't seem to make their shoes match their pants, I still find myself falling for them—over and over and over again.

Blame It on Cinderella

For as long as I can remember, I have been fascinated by the idea that a man and a woman can fall in love with each other. It all started with some kind of chemical imbalance in me that caused a weakness for enchanted castles and glass slippers.

When I was growing up, all of my favorite picture books included a princess in distress and some magical sprinkle dust. When I was in grade school, I sang songs about a mermaid who fell in love with a human prince and then sacrificed her voice for a pair of legs.

As a teenager I considered myself too mature for cartoon nonsense, and I began to appreciate stories that were a little more believable—for example, two strangers falling in love before having a chance meeting atop the Empire State Building on Valentine's Day. My refined taste only lasted for a little while, though. I just couldn't get by without Disney. As a young adult I let go of all my pretensions and went back to enjoying *Beauty and the Beast*.

I just can't help being fascinated with love. I grin during weddings, and my eyes get teary every time I watch *While You Were Sleeping*. I become giddy during televised marriage proposals, and I go nuts inside every time a guy starts singing along with his guitar.

I'll readily admit that my fascination with love causes flighty reactions to everyday romance. But even more than that, my fascination with love makes me hope that there could be a man out there somewhere who might fall for me someday, a man who will bring me my very own fairy tale.

Some Kind of Muffin

My dad robbed the cradle when he married my mom. He was twenty-one years old when he first laid eyes on her, and she was only sixteen. He had graduated from high school three years earlier, and she still had two years left. Despite their age difference, though, things worked out between them.

Which is odd, I guess, considering the way it all began.

My mom likes to say that my dad was the most eligible bachelor in town. He was active in his church, and he was the star shortstop on a local fast-pitch softball team. He was intelligent and well-spoken, and he was a hard worker too. He came from a good family, he had his own savings account, and he could outrun almost anybody in a footrace. And he drove a motorcycle.

My dad met my mom when her family started attending the church that he attended. The first time he saw her, she was walking across the church parking lot. (I know—it's not very romantic, is it?)

At the time my mom was having knee problems, so she had to use crutches, and one of her legs was in a huge brace. To make things even more difficult, as she walked she was trying to keep her skirt from being blown up in the wind.

But, alas, it was *very* windy, and her skirt was *very* short. (What can I say? It was the seventies.) With one strong gust of wind, my mom had my dad's full attention.

That was the easy part. For the next few weeks my dad had to do some serious work to get my mom's attention. For example, at a church potluck dinner, he ate so many of the bran muffins she had baked that he practically threw up. And she didn't even notice him.

After a few more embarrassing attempts of that sort, my dad gave up trying to be subtle. He got on his motorcycle, drove over to my mom's house, and asked her out.

Whenever I hear my mom and dad's story retold, I can't help but smile. I love trying to picture my mom with her crutches and her short skirt and her massive knee brace. I love trying to picture my dad driving a motorcycle. I love the fact that he practically puked at a church function. But more than anything, I love the fact that he fell for her.

Spinning and Searching

I have always wondered what it would feel like to be the girl whom a guy fell for. I have always wondered what it would be like to have someone who would make himself sick on bran muffins for me. I have always hoped that someday I would understand the feeling, that someday someone amazing would fall for me.

But I have this recurring nightmare that makes it hard to hope too much. In my nightmare I'm surrounded by all the men in the universe, and as I look around me, I don't see *him*. I don't see *my* guy—the one who has been reserved especially to fall for me.

I crane my neck to see above the crowd, and then I stand up on tiptoes to see even farther. Shading my eyes from the sun's rays, I lift my chin and look out across the tip of my nose. Faces surround me everywhere, but I still can't see *him*.

I scan the crowd in a slow, 360-degree turn, letting my gaze pass over each face before me. Every face is blank. I squint and do another turn. *He must be here, right?* I think to myself. I do another turn, but I still can't spot him.

I begin to get a little panicky. *This can't be true,* I tell myself, spinning faster with each rotation. *He has got to be here somewhere!*

I spin faster and faster, spinning and searching. But the faces before me remain blank and empty. *He* is not there.

On Tiptoe

I wish I could tell you that waking up from such a nightmare is relieving for me. I wish I could tell you that the minute I open my eyes everything always feels better. It doesn't. In fact, I often find it difficult to believe that I have really woken up at all.

As I look around me and observe the guys in my life, there are many times when I feel that I should be craning my neck and standing on tiptoe for a better view. No matter how many faces are before me, none of them seem to be that one face that I've been looking for.

So I spin and I search, and I spin and I search—and unlike the "me" in my nightmare, I begin to get dizzy. I get tired of all my searching, and my neck gets sore from all its craning. I drop down from my tiptoes, and I begin to ponder my options in this sea of blank faces.

Maybe I'm being too picky, I think to myself. *Maybe I should relax my expectations a little.* I slowly get back up on my tiptoes, with newly relaxed expectations in mind. I scan the crowd once more, and this time a few faces stand out.

Excited, I begin to approach those men who finally seem to fit the bill. *This could be it!* I tell myself, quickening my pace. *This could be the day!*

But as I get nearer and nearer, my confidence wavers—because I know in my heart that this is *not* the day. I am sure of it. I have known it all along, really, because not one of the men before me is the kind of man I have dreamed of.

Dangerous Dreaming

Before I started planning my First Kiss Party, I didn't let myself dream about Prince Charming very much. I wanted to dream about him, but every time I started to, I would get scared. As Erma Bombeck once wrote, "I hid my dreams in the back of my mind—it was the only safe place in the house. From time to time I would get them out and play with them, not daring to reveal them to anyone else because they were so fragile and might get broken."

That's exactly how I felt whenever I dreamed about my Prince Charming. Every now and then I would let myself entertain a few romantic notions about him, but just as quickly I would dismiss those notions, banishing them from my thoughts. It was just too dangerous to dream the way I dreamed.

I have this uncanny ability to get attached to my hopes and aspirations, you see. No matter how silly my dreams may be, once I get them in my head it's very difficult to make them disappear.

So I was deathly afraid that if I dreamed about Mr. Right too hard or too long or too much, I might not ever find a real person who could live up to all my dreams. I figured that the more I pictured one specific ideal, the less likely I was to find someone who would seem good enough.

Before I started planning my First Kiss Party, I was correct about one thing in this matter of dreaming. I was correct when I assumed that a person could dream too much about Mr. Right. I was correct when I figured that a person could dream unrealistically about Prince Charming. As I read somewhere, "The perfect man is a romantic fiction. He doesn't exist."

If I let myself dream to the point where I cannot accept any flaws in a man, I have definitely dreamed too far. No one should expect to find a mate who is 100 percent loving and charming and fun and brilliant and athletic. That kind of guy just isn't going to happen. As my friend Katie points out, "Even the greatest guys can't live up to every expectation."

So I was right on that one thing. But that was where my right-ness ended.

The Stash and the Dream

Just because it's possible to dream *too much* doesn't mean that we shouldn't dream *at all.* (That's no fun!)

In the same way, just because it's possible to be *unrealistic* doesn't mean that it's impossible to be *realistic.* We can develop some kind of expectations for our Prince Charming. Let's face it: Nobody wants to end up with that guy who picks his nose and doesn't brush his teeth.

When I began planning things for my First Kiss Party, it shocked me to discover how much fun it was to think about the man of my dreams. I was amazed at how great it was to imagine actually meeting him someday. I was thrilled at the idea that I might be able to throw a party because of his kiss. As my excitement grew, I slowly began to let myself dream.

At first I dreamed about silly things, like "I hope he's taller than I am." I dreamed of watching him smile and hearing him laugh. I dreamed of knowing the color of his eyes, and I dreamed of knowing how my hand would feel in his. I dreamed of playing "footsie" with him under a dining room table, and I dreamed of watching him stand at the end of a church aisle, all dressed up in a tuxedo and an ascot tie.

Basically, I just dreamed of him. But then, as my dreams of Prince Charming became a regular part of my life, something changed.

I ran across a verse in the Bible: "A wife of noble character is her husband's crown" (Proverbs 12:4). I read the verse once, then I stopped and read it again: "A wife of noble character is her husband's crown."

For the first time ever it hit me. All along I had been dreaming about my dream guy, my future husband, but I had hardly ever dreamed about myself as his future wife.

Let Him Be Like You

Ruth Bell is best known today by her married name: Ruth Bell Graham, the wife of evangelist Billy Graham. She and Billy are such a dynamic duo today that it would be easy to forget that the two of them lived very separate lives at one time.

When Ruth Bell was growing up, she was the daughter of missionaries in China. She was deeply committed to serving God on the mission field there, and she had hardly any desire to marry. When she became a young woman, though, her desires changed just a little.

Ruth began to wonder if marriage might be in her future, and she began to dream about the possibility of having a husband one day. And then she really started dreaming about him. One day, as she traveled by boat from China to America—only a few years before she met Billy Graham—Ruth wrote a prayer about her future mate. In the form of a beautiful poem, she expressed her heart's true desire for a husband: someone not necessarily handsome or wealthy or strong. What she wanted that day was a man whose face showed character and whose soul had been refined—someone whose life was a reflection of Christ.

It comes as no surprise that a young woman like Ruth Bell was the one whom Billy Graham chose. It comes as no surprise because, even way back then, Ruth had a heart almost exactly like the heart that made her husband famous: a heart that was devoted to God first and foremost. And because her heart was so devoted, she would not even consider marrying a man whose heart wasn't similarly devoted.

Not only was Ruth Bell *looking* for the man of her dreams, but she was *being* the kind of woman whom the man of her dreams was looking for.

Dreams of the Heart

As Ruth's story shows, the condition of your heart has a big effect on the results of your dreams. The qualities that you seek to find in Mr. Right say a lot about the qualities that you yourself have to offer.

And so I ask: What kind of man are you dreaming about? What kind of heart are you dreaming of? Are you dreaming about someone who loves the Lord with all his heart, or are you dreaming about someone who looks good in a button-down shirt? Are you dreaming about someone with character, or are you dreaming about someone with cash?

If we are wise, we are looking for the man who loves the Lord and has character. Now, tell me this: What kind of woman is that man looking for?

Do you love God the way that you want your husband to love God? Are you as pure as you want him to be? Are you as faithful as you want him to be? Are you as loving as you want him to be?

Are you strong enough to wait for someone great? Are you trusting enough to think that God might have somebody amazing for you? Are you bold enough to believe that you deserve somebody amazing?

Don't let yourself fall in love with somebody just to say that you've fallen in love. Wait and hope for the kind of guy you dream of.

Don't let your age or your circumstances diminish the way that you dream. Wait and hope.

Don't lower your standards just so you can have a guy on your arm and a vase full of flowers on your dresser. Wait and hope.

Don't let your fear make you ignore the deepest dreams in your heart. Wait and hope.

A Completely Different Place

If it had been up to me, I would have fallen in love long ago. In fact, I would have chosen to fall in love over almost anything else—hands down. I wanted to have my share of candlelight dinners. I wanted to have dozens of roses sent to my door. I wanted albums full of lovey pictures. And I wanted some kisses of my own.

I never intended to have things turn out the way that they have for me. I never hoped to be dateless all through high school, and none of my dreams for the future included being a twenty-year-old with virgin lips.

It's funny how life can get a hold of you, though, and suddenly you find yourself in a completely different place from where you thought you would be. Today, as I stand on the "other side" of my teen years, I find it weird that I haven't been in a romantic relationship. It feels strange, somehow, that I can legally vote, and yet I'm still waiting to get asked out on a date. And it's extremely odd for me to comprehend that, as a twenty-year-old, I still wonder what a kiss feels like.

Even so, when I step back and evaluate the life that I'm living today, I can honestly say that I wouldn't have it any other way. Although I haven't fallen in love yet, things are going all right for me. Although I haven't fallen in love, I've been dreaming about it, and that has made all the difference.

Him

My dream guy has a quick smile and a great sense of humor; in fact, he can make me laugh really, really hard. He has enough confidence to walk with his head held high, and he has enough humility to ask forgiveness when he's wrong. He is goofy, so he is willing to sit on the floor with a three-year-old. He is considerate, so he notices the girl who always sits in the corner by herself.

My guy has a romantic side that will bring him to my

doorstep armed with a handful of flowers that he picked on his way over. He is intelligent enough to know what a preposition is, and he is gracious enough to explain its meaning to someone who doesn't. He has a solid group of male friends, and more of them than female friends.

Now, since all of the things that I've listed so far are pretty noble characteristics, allow me to squeeze in just one superficial dream. My dream guy is about four inches taller than my five-foot-ten frame. (I have always wanted to fit snugly underneath my man's shoulder. And call me shallow, but I just *love* wearing my high heels.) OK, that's it for the superficial stuff. Thanks for indulging me.

My ideal guy cherishes my purity and values me enough to wait for it. He doesn't think it's dorky that I'm planning a First Kiss Party. (After all, he gets to have the first kiss!) He is discerning, he is respected by his peers, and he remembers his mom's birthday. He is a spiritual leader, and he seeks to be a disciple of his Lord.

He really is quite the guy, isn't he?!

Happily Ever Before

I hope and pray that my Prince Charming is out there somewhere. I don't think that he has found me yet. Despite that fact, I am enjoying my time waiting for him, because I am convinced that he is worth waiting for (even if he is just a figment of my imagination).

As I wait for him, I am learning how to be the kind of woman whom he will be looking for. I am learning how to grow in grace, wisdom, strength, purity, and godly character. Slowly but surely I am working to become the woman that I want to be—the kind of woman whom the man of my dreams will fall madly in love with.

And every now and then, when I'm dreaming about him, I make a little trip to the store and check out the decorations aisle just for fun. As I look over the supply of balloons and streamers and noisemakers and cake toppers, I am reminded of why I keep all that confetti in my closet.

Maybe, just maybe, the guy I've been dreaming about really *does* exist out there somewhere. *Maybe, just maybe, he dreams about me the way I dream about him.*

And who knows? As I happily peruse the decorations aisle, *he* could be falling in love with my smile.

Notes

Chapter Two
Great White Spaces

1. Eric and Leslie Ludy, *When God Writes Your Love Story* (Sisters, Ore.: Loyal, 1999), 131.

Chapter Three
A Not-So Leap of Faith

1. Oswald Chambers, *My Utmost for His Highest*, February 22.
2. "Song of Songs' Theme and Theology," Notes in the *NIV Study Bible* (Grand Rapids, Mich.: Zondervan, 2000), 1003.
3. Song of Songs 2:7b; 3:5b; 8:4b.
4. George Meredith, "Love in the Valley."
5. Proverbs 14:29a.
6. Psalm 27:14.

Chapter Four
No More Cheese, Please

1. C.S. Lewis, *Mere Christianity* (London: Macmillan, 1980), 54.
2. Jaci Velasquez, "When I Feel Lonely," *Campus Life* (January/February 2000), www.christianitytoday.com/cl/2000/001/

3. Psalm 57:10.
4. Max Lucado, *When God Whispers Your Name* (Dallas: Word, 1994), 179.

Chapter Five
Mirror, Mirror

1. Ephesians 2:10, NLT.
2. 1 Samuel 16:7.
3. 1 Peter 3:3-4.
4. Kim Boyce, quoted in Andrea Stephens, *Happy Thoughts for Bad Hair Days* (Ann Arbor, Mich.: Servant, 2001), 50.
5. Beverly Patchin, "The Eye of the Beholder," *Boundless Webzine* (November 14, 2002). www.boundless.org/2000/features/a0000317.html
6. Mitch Albom, *Tuesdays With Morrie* (New York: Doubleday, 1997), 120.
7. 2 Corinthians 5:12.

Chapter Six
A Little Black Dress

1. Nate Combs, quoted by Susie Shellenberger, "Plus One Rides With Brio," *Brio Magazine* (April 2001), 23.
2. Rory Partin, "Straight From a Guy," *Brio Magazine* (November 2001).
3. Wendy Shalit, *A Return to Modesty: Discovering the Lost Virtue* (New York: Touchstone, 2002), 182.

4. Laurie Schecter, quoted by Linda Sunshine and Mary Tiegreen, *A Passion for Shoes* (Kansas City: Andrews McMeel, 1995), 21.

Chapter Seven
That Girl

1. Steve DeNeff, "The Secret Place," sermon at College Wesleyan Church, Marion, Ind., January 13, 2002.

Chapter Eight
The Missing Piece

1. Dan Seaborn, *26 Words That Will Improve the Way You Do Family* (Ann Arbor, Mich.: Servant, 2002), 141.
2. Lewis, 94.
3. Martha Bolton, *If The Pasta Wiggles, Don't Eat It!* (Ann Arbor, Mich.: Servant, 1995), 107.

Chapter Nine
Purple Stuff and Other Extras

1. Lewis, 90.
2. Dannah Gresh, *And the Bride Wore White: The Seven Secrets to Sexual Purity* (Chicago: Moody, 2000), 90.
3. Christian Nestell Bovee.
www.brainyquote.com/quotes/authors/c/a126185.html

4. Jason Perry and Steve Keels, *You Are Not Your Own: Living Loud for God* (Nashville: Broadman & Holman, 2002), 46-47.
5. Song of Songs 8:6.
6. Emil Ludwig (1881–1948). Source unknown.
7. Bethany Torode, "Kiss Me Now," *Boundless Webzine* (November 13, 2002). www.boundless.org/2000/departments/beyond_buddies/a0000366.html